Writing Crime Fiction

Making Crime Pay

Janet Laurence

Studymates

ISBN: 978-1-84285-088-6

First published in 2007 by Studymates Limited.
PO Box 225, Abergele, LL18 9AY, United Kingdom.

Website: http://www.studymates.co.uk

Typeset by Vikatan Publishing Solutions, Chennai, India
Printed and bound in Great Britain by Baskerville Press

Writing Crime Fiction

Making Crime Pay

Studymates academic books

Algebra: Basic Algebra Explained
Better English
Better French
Better French 2
Better German
Better Spanish
British History 1870-1918
Chemistry: chemistry calculations explained
European History
Genetics
Hitler & Nazi Germany
Lenin, Stalin and Communist Russia
Mathematics for adults
Organic Chemistry
Plant Physiology
Poems to Live By
Poetry
Practical Drama
Shakespeare
Social Anthropology
Study skills
The Academic Essay
The English Reformation
The New Science Teacher's Handbook
The War Poets
Understanding Maths
Warfare

Studymates Writers Guides

Kate Walker's 12-Point Guide to Writing Romance
Starting to Write
The Business of Writing
Writing Crime Fiction
Writing Historical Fiction
Writing How to books
Writing Travel
Writing Tv Scripts

Studymates Post-Graduate Guides

Your Masters Thesis
Your PhD Thesis

Many other titles in preparation

Contents

Foreword by Val McDermid   xi

Introduction   xiii
     What is a crime novel?   xiii

1   Getting Started   1
     Plotting & Ideas   1
     Exercise   3
     Conflict and suspense   6
     Exercise   6
     All the news that can't be printed   8
     Looking behind facts   9
     Exercise   11
     What sort of story will you be comfortable writing?   12
     Fairy tales – the truth   12
     Exercise   13
     Sub-plots   15
     Exercise   16
     Using specialised knowledge   16
     So now get started   17
     Plotting & ideas   17

2   Choosing An Approach and Dealing With Outlines   19
     Different approaches   19
     Exercise   19
     Categories of crime novel   19
     Discovering what sells   23
     Exercise   24
     Your sort of crime novel   25
     Exercise   26
     Outlines – are they needed?   28
     Advantages of an outline   28
     Disadvantages of an outline   30
     Forms of outline   31

Exercise   33
Approaches & outlines   35

3   **Settings and Issues**   **37**
Settings   37
Uses of settings   39
Choosing a setting   40
Exercise   40
Issues   43
Exercise   44
Exercise   46
Issues can be buried or ignored   46
Settings & issues   47

4   **Characterisation and Motivation**   **49**
Exercise   50
Exercise   53
Descriptions   56
Body language   59
Behaviour   60
Exercise   60
Possessions   61
Names   62
Characterisation & motivation   64

5   **Dialogue**   **67**
Exercise   67
Exercise   70
Eavesdropping   71
Using dialogue to develop plot   72
Exercise   72
Make information interesting   73
Relax or tighten tension   74
Accents   75
Historical dialogue   75
Read dialogue out loud   78
Exercise   79
Dialogue   79

6   **Backgrounds and Specialist Knowledge**   **81**
    Specialist backgrounds & series characters   81
    Does the amateur sleuth have a place in the modern
        crime novel?   82
    Looking for tension and discord   86
    Specialised knowledge   87
    Murder methods & forensic science   87
    Exercise   87
    Descriptions of death   88
    Poison as a murder weapon   92
    Make sure of details   93
    Police investigations   93
    Exercise   95
    Backgrounds & specialist knowledge   95

7   **Narrative Style and First Paragraphs**   **97**
    Point of view   97
    Choosing a voice   97
    First person narrator   97
    Third person narration   100
    Exercise   101
    Switching point of view   101
    Show don't tell   104
    Exercise   104
    Creating an individual style   106
    First paragraphs   107
    Exercise   108
    Exercise   112
    Rewriting first paragraphs   112
    How literary can a crime novel be?   112
    Narrative style & first paragraphs   113

8   **Focus, Suspects, Clues and Red Herrings**   **115**
    Changing the focus or following the trail   116
    Exercise   118
    Shifting the point of view   118
    Voices from the grave   120
    Exercise   121

Voices within   121
Number of suspects   122
Exercise   123
Series character   123
Clues   124
Clues of inference   125
Clues in lists   126
Two-way clues   127
Two-part clues   128
Red herrings   128
Exercise   129
Focus, suspects, clues & red herrings   129

9   **Pace or The Smoking Gun**   **131**
Questions   131
Chapter hooks   132
Exercise   133
Pace   133
Less is more   135
Exercise   136
Reducing exposition   137
Skipping over time   138
Opening with a bang   139
Continuing with fireworks   140
Pace or the smoking gun   141

10 **Denouements and Endings**   **143**
The magic 'w's.   144
Keeping true to the book   147
Denouements   147
Tie up sub-plots   149
Exercise   149
Writing the ending   149
The final check   150
The end   152
Exercise   153
Denouements & endings   153

11 **Research** 155

Location 155
Exercise 158
Historical locations 158
Background 160
Technical questions 160
Medical detail 161
Police procedure 162
Forensic information 164
Pictures 166
Exercise 167
Indentifying research 167
Verification 168
Research 168

12 **Selling Your Book** 169

Length 169
Title 170
Final manuscript checks 172
Format 173
Selling your book 175
Basic guidelines 175
Points to get over 177
Covering letter 178
Synopsis 178
Curriculum vitae 179
Exercise 180
The Crime Writers' Association Debut Dagger 180
Other options 181
Keep writing 182
Selling your book 185

Appendix I 187
Useful Books 187

Appendix II 189

Acknowledgements 193

Index 197

Foreword
by Val McDermid

Photo courtesy of
www.valmcdermid.com

Back in the 1920s, both British and American writers compiled lists of rules for writing detective novels. They forbade such devices as twins, solutions arriving in dreams and, for some reason, Chinamen. They laid down a straitjacket of conventions that would-be writers were supposed to follow.

They'd have drummed me out of the club.

For me, one of the delights of writing crime fiction these days is that there are no rules and no limits. Since I published my first book, *Report for Murder*, in 1987, a new generation of writers has transformed the genre and opened up the widest possible range of storytelling possibilities. For the writer, these new horizons have made writing crime fiction far more exciting than ever before. There is room in this broad church for every flavour of mystery.

I started to write crime novels because I'd always enjoyed reading them – and because the New Wave of American women crime writers made me wonder if I could write something similar set in the UK. I quickly realised that I could write about anyone, anywhere, in any context. In the twenty years since that first novel, I have produced a wide variety of crime books ranging from dark psychological thrillers to wisecracking private eye novels. My inspirations have stretched from land law to the mutiny on the Bounty, via medieval torture and feminist politics. I've written three different series as well as several stand-alone books. I like the challenge of trying something new and flexing my writing muscles

WRITING CRIME FICTION will teach you to flex your writing muscles. It looks at every aspect of the crime novel and offers guidance on developing your own voice so that you can tell the stories that clamour in your heart and your head. As I said, there are no rules, but there are certainly expectations.

Working through this book will prove an ideal introduction to the creative process that lies behind producing a book that readers will want to read and a publisher will want to publish.

One of the other delights of writing crime fiction is my colleagues. I don't think there is another section of the literary world where the practitioners are both so sociable and so supportive. We actually enjoy each other's work and respect each other's talents. That's why so many of my fellow members of the Crime Writers' Association have offered advice here. From them you will learn key tricks of the trade, and the most important lesson of all – that every author must find the way of working that suits them best. Only you know the sort of book you want to produce; WRITING CRIME FICTION will help you identify how to make it a success.

This book looks at all the areas a crime writer needs to consider. What makes a book a crime novel? How do you choose the right approach for your story? What motivates your criminal? How do you create and sustain tension? What is a successful conclusion? What part does research play? All these matters and many more are dealt with. There are exercises to fire your creative impulses and help your voice to develop.

Writing takes commitment and hard work. Nobody gets it right first time but the more you write, the more you learn. Unlock your imagination and start on the journey to telling your unique story with its engaging characters set against an atmospheric backdrop. Good luck!

Val McDermid

Introduction

Crime novels are always popular. Libraries offer well-stocked shelves that contain nothing but crime fiction. Bookshops have sections devoted to new additions to the genre as well as the previously published novels of the most popular authors. Crime writers such as Val McDermid, Ian Rankin, and Minette Walters head best-seller lists.

Publishers are eager to find new writers who can be equally successful and the crime genre offers the writer a wide range of approaches and types of story to choose from.

Don't, however, make the mistake of thinking it is easy. There are no guarantees in life and that holds particularly true for the publishing world. The important thing to remember is that the possibilities are there; it's a market looking for new products and why shouldn't you be the one to offer what it wants? All you may need is a little help.

That is what this book is all about. We are going to look at the whole process of producing a successful crime novel, from where a good idea first comes from, developing it into a workable plot, through to the importance of characterisation, motive, dialogue, pace and denouement. Along the way we will also look at the unique battle the crime novel conducts between author and reader, how it can seduce and delude before the final mysteries are revealed.

What is a crime novel?

Crime and Punishment is one of the greatest books by the Russian novelist, Dostoevsky. It is accepted as a piece of classic literature. The same can be said of books written by Edgar Allan Poe and Wilkie Collins. These nineteenth century writers looked at what drives a human being to crime, how both the perpetrator and others are affected by such an act, and how the criminal can be discovered and brought to justice. All the elements that are explored by today's crime writers.

The twenties and thirties are looked on as the classic age for the crime novel. Agatha Christie's books are still in print, as are those of Dorothy Sayers, Margery Allingham and Ngaio Marsh. They set the standard that many others tried to emulate.

For the most part the so-called Golden Age crime novels portray a world of house parties, intellectual pursuits, Riviera jaunts and the sort of society that relies on others to make sure they are comfortable and able to live their preferred life. A life that bore very little relation to that of some ninety per cent of the population.

In these books suspects were numerous, the investigator was an amateur (let's exclude Ngaio Marsh and her Chief Inspector Alleyne) and too often the police were bumbling incompetents. Most of the suspense was involved with the contradictions uncovered by the investigation: alibis, locked rooms and other puzzling elements. It was more a case of howdunnit and whodunit rather than whydunnit. Apart from those of the greats mentioned above, the books were as much puzzles as mysteries.

It took Raymond Chandler and Dashiell Hammet to show that there could be another side to the crime novel. The emergence of Philip Marlowe, Chandler's high principled but cynical and world-weary private eye was a revelation. Authors such as Elmore Leonard and Ed McBain followed along the road that Chandler and Hammet had outlined.

In Europe and South America, authors used the crime novel to explore political and social injustice and unrest. Many writers working in dictator regimes have trod a narrow path through the dangers of imprisonment.

In the United Kingdom, however, it took a long time for the crime novel to become more than an entertainment. Often witty, clever and thought-provoking, with authors capable of deep insights into human nature, the genre only gradually looked beyond middle class society.

The nineties, though, saw the emergence of the crime novel that explored social issues and was not afraid to go beyond entertainment. The contemporary crime novel is much more than a puzzle. To be successful, it has to work as a general novel. Its characters have to be believable, the plot has to involve the reader beyond a simple mystery level, and the writing needs to fire the reader's imagination. It will also contain a number of features that place it firmly in the crime genre:

- First and most obviously, the story has to concern a crime. The crime most usually, but not always, is murder. When the death penalty existed, stories often involved the detective in a race against the hangman; could the accused be proven innocent in time to save their life? A period crime novel can still offer this suspense. Today, however, murder is most often chosen because the taking of life is the ultimate, most heinous of crimes. However, not every crime novel centres round murder. Theft, blackmail, fraud, for instance, can provide ways of putting characters under the sort of pressure that produces an involving plot.

- Secondly, a crime novel offers a mystery that needs unravelling. There may be thrills and spills along the way but the plot will involve an investigation. One of the reasons I believe crime novels are popular is that readers love the structure: A crime is committed, the mystery of why and by whom is investigated, the reader is challenged to solve the mystery before the denouement and, at the end, the solution is revealed and just desserts are handed out to the perpetrator. There are any number of variations on this theme, including the perpetrator avoiding the penalty of their crime, but it is closely followed by the majority of crime novels.

- The crime novel includes a victim(s), an investigator, and several suspects. The number can vary; too few and the reader may be able to work out who 'did it' too early, too many and the reader – not to mention the author – can get confused.

- I mentioned above the challenge that a crime novel offers to the reader – to discover 'whodunnit' before the book reveals the perpetrator. While a successful novel often depends on keeping the reader turning the pages to discover what happens next; with a crime novel, the reader assumes that there is a puzzle and there will be clues offered that can help solve it – or bamboozle the unwary into following a false trail, the famous 'red herrings'. Agatha Christie, that master of the twisty plot and the burying of vital clues, is sometimes blamed today for a lack of development in her characters. Today's author has to remember that the story must arise from the characters involved. Colonel Plum in the library with the candlestick may do for the board game *Cluedo;* it won't work for a publisher.

- Finally, there has to be a resolution. Many of today's most successful crime novels work on a number of different levels but by the end the reader has to be satisfied that all the various strands have been brought together and the crime's perpetrator revealed.

So, a crime novel is a story with a crime, a mystery as to who did it and why, and an investigation that will reveal these answers. It will offer the reader a variety of suspects and alternative solutions, and, hopefully, an unexpected but completely satisfying denouement. It will have believable and interesting characters, a plot that engages the reader, suspects with a variety of motivations, and it will have 'pace' that will keep the reader turning the pages until THE END is reached.

This book takes a look at how you can write a successful crime novel.

To help me, I turned to some of our leading crime writers for the advice they could offer to new budding authors in the genre. Their words of wisdom appear throughout this book. As well, I recommend studying crime writer's websites, many include fascinating accounts of how they started and where the ideas for certain books came from; Ian Rankin's is particularly good. Many also contain illuminating articles on them and their work.

Let's begin this book with some general comments from writers and publishers who provided advice. I'll start with what I think can be seen as an ideal recipe for writing a successful crime book. It's from Hilary Hale, a doyenne of literary editors, who bought my first book. She talks about the publisher's task:

'When taking on a new writer, publishers consider the long term prospects of an author's career as much as the quality of their first book. Strong story-telling, a central character readers can identify with and care about, a convincing background, and a plot which stretches the imagination and the intellect are extremely important, but the investment a publisher has to make to establish an author within the trade means that they need to know that the author will deliver new books regularly (one a year is the ideal) which are of a similar genre. Novels with a series character are the most popular with readers and enable a backlist to stay 'alive' longer than a series of 'one-offs', though a series can be linked by place or profession rather than a single character. Always try to be different, not just follow the fashion of the bestselling lists.'

Ian Rankin never did a creative writing course, never bought a 'How To' book and had plenty of rejection letters along the way. 'Even when I had six or seven books published, I was still always on the verge of being dropped. I guess you need self-belief; you need a thick skin (to deal with the rejection letters). You need patience and commitment and quite a bit of luck. And it helps to know your market.'

Here is some advice on a place to work, 'Create the best preconditions for you. Anyone with a background in journalism is used to working cheek by jowl with dozens of other people but most of us need solitude. A room of our own is therefore vital. Make sure it's equipped with all that you need.' That is from Keith Miles, who also writes as Edward Marston.

Not everyone is able to dedicate a room to their writing but there are other ways of making a space in which to work. Remember J K Rowling and how she wrote the first Harry Potter novel at a table in a café. A library can provide a quiet environment in which to write. At home, a desk in a bedroom or a corner in the kitchen can work well. What is important is being able to go to the same place every day, and have your subconscious know that now you are in the place where you do your writing. If you can keep your computer or your writing tools there plus your reference books, so much the better. As soon as you sit down and switch the machine on or pick up your pen, your mind should already be attuned to work.

Keith Miles also says, 'Talent is not enough. You must have the stamina to exploit and extend it. Self-discipline is the key here. To build up your stamina, set yourself a strict writing schedule and keep to it. Writing a full-length novel is a marathon. Get yourself fit enough to complete the course.' He adds what can be seen as a warning, 'Read the copyright laws.'

The advice on writing something every day is something we will come back to. Peter Lovesey says, 'I'm a deplorably slow writer but a page a day becomes a substantial novel in a year.' Breaking the task down in this way makes it achievable. Everyone can do a page a day. Keep doing that and in a year you will have a book.

Liz Evans suggests, 'Write what you want to write – rather than what you think you ought to write. It's no good setting out to write a cut and slash thriller if you hate them. You'll get bored and it will show in your writing. The easiest bits of the book are "Chapter One" and "The End". It's the stuff in between that's hard. Remember that the excuses not to start writing will always expand to fill the time available if you let them.'

Martin Edwards agrees, 'The most important thing about writing a crime novel, just as for any other sort of novel, is that you want to write it more than anything else.'

Michael Jecks urges writers to, 'Always, always carry a notepad with you. You will get ideas in concerts, in the pub, in the street, out walking the dog, while sitting in front of the TV – everywhere. Never let an idea go without writing it down, because if you do, you will forget it; note it, store it, and keep the idea in a box nearby. When you're at a loss for ideas, go back to it and sort through old ideas. It'll invariably get you going.'

Paula Gosling defines the very special appeal of a crime novel, 'Crime fiction writers today produce novels that are as rich in characterisation, setting, and theme as any other form of literature. But there is something more, something unique to crime fiction, and that is the unspoken contract between author and reader. It is a direct face-to-face confrontation. The author offers a novel that contains a puzzle, and the reader wants to solve that puzzle. The duel continues throughout the book, the author offering clues in as many guises as possible, the reader trying to discern and connect each one beneath the narrative. In an ideal situation the reader arrives at the solution just before the author reveals it, thereby satisfying both that they have played the game successfully. And that is why it's so satisfying to write and to read a good "mystery".

A final piece of advice from Lindsey Davis, 'Don't drink and type. The films are wrong. You will never write your masterpiece with the aid of a bottle of rye. You need every ounce of sobriety to master your spell-checker.'

1 Getting Started

Plotting & Ideas

This chapter is all about getting together ideas that will provide the basis for a plot.

In talking about plot, the great crime writer, H R F Keating, once said that E M Forster defines a story as a narrative of events with the emphasis falling on causality. 'The king died and then the queen died' is a story. 'The king died and then queen died of grief' is a plot. But: 'The queen died, no one knew why, until it was discovered that it was through grief at the death of the king' that is a plot with a mystery in it, a form capable of high development.

There you have it, in the judgement of Forster, one of the most respected of English novelists; plots with mysteries in them are capable of high development.

What is a good mystery plot? One that keeps readers guessing. One that involves strong emotions and motives: jealousy, greed, redemptive love, revenge, sacrifice. One that has characters that involve the reader. One in which the reader can recognise conflicts and settings.

The elements of a plot, though, are not enough to make a successful book.

Reginald Hill says, 'plotting is not the story you want to tell, it is finding the best way of telling that story'.

Before, though, we look at ways of getting a plot down on the page, let's see where we go for the ideas that will, eventually, lead to a plot.

Many people ask authors, 'Where do you get your ideas?' It's almost as though they think there's a shop that offers them for sale, its location known only to writers. It's a nice thought. How much, I wonder, would such ideas cost?

In fact, ideas are free, they are everywhere; you just have to open your mind to them.

Dealing with the question where ideas come from, Jessica Mann says, 'There are as many answers as there are writers.

Some have an endless stream of notions popping into their heads. Mine come more slowly, usually appearing when I'm not looking for them, so between books I worry that there will never be another. Then something begins to niggle.'

Plot ideas sometimes arrive fully formed. Wonderful if that happens. More often, though, plots are put together like a jigsaw puzzle: a bit here, a piece there, all gradually built up until there is a workable whole. Maybe a character or a set of characters starts the process off, or it may be a setting. Perhaps it's an idea for a crime, or an alibi. Or an incident you read about, or something that happens to you.

Peter Lovesey says his initial idea 'can come from anywhere. Sometimes it's background, a character, a theme, but usually the plot. For instance the inspiration for *Rough Cider* came from a non-fiction book on cider making. I read that they hung a joint of meat inside the barrel of cider to assist fermentation. That got my criminal mind working, and I thought, instead of a leg of lamb in there, suppose it was a skull that turned up?'

A good way to start plotting is to ask questions. Like any successful novel, a crime story will constantly pose questions. What has happened? Who is that person and why are they behaving in that way? The readers keep turning the pages to find out answers. In a crime novel there are two different sorts of questions:

a) Firstly, there are the questions that have to be asked as part of an investigation: What was the crime, where did it happen, when did it happen, how was it done, who did it and why? Your plot has to take all of these questions into consideration and the answers need to be fed out gradually, with misunderstandings, wrong conclusions and alternative solutions offered along the way, together with clues and evidence that can point first one way and then another, until the final denouement is reached.

b) Then there are the questions that may or may not be relevant to the investigation but will make the reader want to know more – and so keep turning the pages. Why does the sultry Mrs Brown keep disappearing every

Wednesday night? Why has nervous Miss Smith moved somewhere else when she said she was so happy where she was? Why does the unbearably pompous Mr Johnson always avoid meeting high-flying Miss Jones? Why is shy Mrs Thomas, married to a leading councillor, so badly bruised?

Exercise

Write down six questions that an investigator, whether official or un-official, might ask in the early pages of a crime novel dealing with the death of Mary, a forty-year old woman, found lying in her sitting room, dead from a blow to the head. Look beyond the actual facts of the death and think of simple situations that would raise questions that could develop the plot.

There are no right or wrong answers to the exercises set in this book; they are to get you thinking and working along the lines needed for a successful crime novel.

A word of caution here, do not throw away your exercises. You may need to refer back to them later in this book, or you may find that, as you work through the various chapters, that at least some of your answers can be used in a full-length story.

When I was starting out I attended a creative writing course. My first book, *A Deepe Coffyn,* included a number of exercises I produced during this course. As I worked on them, I was soon inspired to think of writing a crime novel. Ideas for the basic plot, the background and some of the characters came to me. So I used each of the tasks we were set: first page, description, dialogue, and so on, to explore possibilities for the book I had dreamed up. Most of what I wrote, suitably tailored, ended up in *A Deepe Coffyn.*

So whether you are writing by hand, using a typewriter, or working on a computer, keep everything you write. Creative work should never be thrown away. It may well come in use later.

Let us look at the exercise you were set.

The questions that could be raised by the imaginary situation given above are only limited by your imagination.

Here is a possible set that the investigator in a crime novel could be faced with:

1) Why had the neighbour who discovered the body gone into the house?
2) What were Mary and her adopted daughter arguing so bitterly about when they were overheard by another neighbour?
3) Why has Mary's husband left her?
4) What has happened to Mary's priceless Ming vase?
5) Who was the mysterious man seen knocking on Mary's door the evening she died?
6) Why the week before her death did Mary buy a one-way ticket to San Francisco, dated for the day after she died?

These are the sorts of questions that can send the investigator – and the reader – off in a number of different directions. The answers to them can reveal a number of different reasons for Mary's death and identify a range of suspects.

Possible answers to the above include:

1) The neighbour might have been given a key to the house by Mary so that her plants could be kept watered while she is away. The neighbour has agreed to take on this task because she believes that Mary is having an affair with her husband and she wants to see if she can find some evidence in the house. When she entered, she thought Mary had already left for San Francisco.
2) Mary and her daughter may have been arguing because the daughter is adopted, she has never got on with Mary, who loves her deeply; she has sought out her birth mother and has decided to move in with her.
3) Mary's husband may have left her because he has come to the point where he cannot handle her gambling addiction any longer. He believes they will soon be facing bankruptcy.
4) The Ming vase could have been sold to buy the ticket to San Francisco and a start to her new life there.

5) The mysterious man could be a debt collector whom Mary attacks when he demands repayment of a loan.
6) Mary sees going to San Francisco, where she has an old boyfriend, as the only way out of the mess that her life has become.

All these characters are frustrated and looking for an escape from a life that has become worse than unsatisfactory. Each of them is desperate enough to become violent to ensure that they can escape.

Mary may have been battered to death by her husband when he discovers that, to pay a gambling debt, she has sold their one last valuable possession, which he was counting on to start him off in a new life. The jealous neighbour might have found proof of an affair and challenged Mary before she was able to leave for San Francisco. Or her daughter could have attacked her because Mary bad-mouthed her birth mother. Mary might have been by hit the debt collector in self-defence when she attacked him.

When I started writing down the questions, nothing of the above was in my mind. I plucked everything out of the air. Then I started to think about answers.

Would what I have sketched out make a book? Not as it stands but maybe it could start me wondering about the conflicts involved: the jealousy between the dead woman and her neighbour; the difficult relationships between parents and adopted children; how gambling can ruin marriages and lives; how anger can lead to violence; the dangers involved in trying to escape the consequences of one's actions.

There could be enough there to start the process of making a plot. Choices would have to be made. Who, for instance, did actually kill Mary and why? What would be the main theme of the plot? Would any of the other suspects play a part or would it be better to keep thinking and digging into Mary and her life? What is the pull gambling has for her? Where does she gamble and whom does she meet in the process?

What questions did you put down? Have you thought about what the answers could be? Could they start you thinking about a possible plot?

Conflict and suspense

Conflict and suspense are essential to a successful crime novel. Conflict creates situations in which something is going to happen, the suspense arises out of being made to wait for the action to occur when it seems obvious that the outcome will be dramatic or dangerous or tragic, or all three.

What can start these twin motors of conflict and suspense?

Exercise

Think of a simple scene in which two people are in conflict. For some reason one has cause to hate the other and tells them why. Now write down a page of dialogue for them. Don't worry about any descriptive comments for each character, just put down their conversation as if you were scripting out a play.

I wrote the following:

'Denise, I'd like to have a word, please. The rest of you, I'll see you at the next aerobics class on Wednesday, right? Now, Denise, you said you were experienced yet it's quite obvious you've never been in an aerobics class in your life before. I think you owe me an explanation.'

'Little white lies never hurt anyone – or do they, Frankie?'

'Certainly they do when it means I don't give you the attention you need as a beginner; you could have damaged yourself.'

'Oh, I've been damaged all right. By you. You see the beginners' class was full and I wanted to meet you. After all, you know my husband very well.'

'Your husband?'

'Peter Morris.'

'Peter's your husband?'

'Last time I checked. Not that you're the first. Nor will be the last.'

'Now, look here, you know nothing about our relationship.'

'No? I think I do. Candlelit dinners at your place, yes? Gifts from abroad, picked up at the airport, because he's always in such a rush? Makes dates and breaks them? Tells you he can't leave his wife at the moment because she's so ill?'

'I....'

'I may not be up to advanced aerobics but I think you can see I'm not an invalid.'

'I don't believe you are Peter's wife.'

'No? Then who am I? Look, Frankie, I think you're an intelligent woman, you're very attractive and you deserve more out of life.'

'If you think you can persuade me to let go of Peter, think again. I don't know what you're up to but he's a wonderful man.'

'That's what I thought, in the beginning. I want you to know what a bastard he is. I think we should get together for a proper chat.'

'Like hell I'll get together with you.'

'Be like that if you want but just think about what that husband of mine is doing to you. You'll come round in the end. You know our number, give me a ring when Peter's at the office but don't leave it too long.'

The reader doesn't know what the wife has in mind. Is she going to murder her rival? Or get her to join in giving the husband a nasty shock, maybe murder him? And what about Frankie, the aerobics teacher? Is she an innocent being seduced by a practised womaniser, or a lonely woman believing she is bringing fulfilment into someone else's life? She might be a *femme fatale* who has met her match. Will she take up Denise's challenge – or try to get rid of her lover's wife?

With my exercise, the reader doesn't know exactly what to think. Your exercise may have been more straightforward. You could have had a character spilling out their hatred and contempt for someone who has injured them. Was the reason for the outburst clear or did you leave questions in the reader's mind that will be answered later? Readers should always have questions in their mind.

However you tackled the exercise, your dialogue should intrigue the reader and make them want to know more about the characters and what has come between them. Is this the start of a confrontation that will escalate? Will it lead to physical violence, even murder?

How much time did you spend working out what the conflict between your two characters was? How it had arisen? Writers have to understand their characters. Then conflict can be developed and with it the potential for suspense.

We will look more closely at characterisation later on. For now, it's back to where ideas for plots can come from.

All the news that can't be printed

Newspapers and magazines are full of ideas for plots. Some newspaper reports can offer an occasional one that seems as though it's perfect just as it is. How about the wife who hired a gunman to shoot her husband? It's also happened the other way round. There are stories of drug gangs in violent bust-ups and major fraud cases. It could be quite easy to think that all you need to do is cut out the story and then write it.

Such an approach has pitfalls.

The first pitfall is very pedestrian but needs heeding. You could run the risk of libel. If your characters are too recognisable, you could be headed for litigation, particularly if the perpetrators fail to be convicted. You need to beware!

More importantly, however, is the need to structure your plot. Think of films made from books and how so much of the time the plot has been altered because a visual media calls for a different structure from one that is literary. It is even more difficult when you try to turn true life into a novel.

As Peter N Walker, who writes the *Heartbeat* novels as Nicholas Rhea, says: 'Plots, of course, can be found anywhere – in the newspapers, on the radio or TV, in conversations between ordinary people, from the imagination or, of course, from one's own experiences. The secret is not to lift the complete plot from real life, but to fictionalise the basic idea then develop it in keeping with your own style and for the attention of your very own detective. One method of devising a plot is to ask the question – "what if?" and then answer it. For example, your local newspaper reports that a funeral parlour was set on fire by an arsonist. As a novelist, ask yourself the question – what if it contained the body of a murder victim? Or murder suspect? Then what happens? And why?'

True life, though, can give you ideas and the sort of stimulation I mentioned earlier.

Be wary of setting a story around drug running or gang cultures. Publishers seem particularly reluctant to take on these novels from first-time novelists. Too few writers truly understand what is involved or can write about such crimes in a way that involves the reader. However, you may have a background that has given you inside knowledge. Maybe you are or have been an investigator in Customs and Excise, perhaps working undercover, for instance; or involved in some way with organised crime; are or have been a police officer. If you can then combine your specialised knowledge with skilful plotting and writing, you may well be onto a winner.

If you lack such specialised knowledge, look for ideas that appeal to you because you can relate to some feature in them. For instance, a description of a character reminds you of someone you know, or a scam is perpetrated in a world you have some experience of, such as antiques or insurance. Try and look behind any news report to what *might* be the real story.

Looking behind facts

There was a report some time ago about a man who signed up to an internet site designed to enable old school friends to get in touch with each other again. He found himself contacted by an old girlfriend and accused of being the biological father of her daughter. The actual facts of the case don't matter. You can use this story as a jumping-off point by asking those magic words, 'what if'?

What if the woman is found dead and the old boyfriend is accused of her murder? He might have had a number of reasons for silencing her. But what if she was trying to blackmail him and he wasn't the only victim? Who else might have wanted her dead? These days DNA tests will sort out paternity questions, so would the woman have accused someone without the accusation being true, or at least her believing it to be true? What if the man *was* the father and was delighted to find out he had a daughter; how would his wife and the children of their marriage feel? Then what if someone else had been trying to track the woman down for some unrelated reason, perhaps because she cheated him out of his share of a business, and the website not only put the woman in touch with her old boyfriend but also enabled the man she'd ruined to catch up with her?

By the end of wondering 'what if', you may have dropped the initial story – that of the ex-boyfriend accused of fathering a child he never knew about, and have developed lots of other ideas. Maybe another news story has added other angles. It's getting started that's important and that's what reading newspapers and magazines, listening to the radio and watching television, especially reality programmes, will do – get you started, allowing you to embroider and build upon an initial idea. What all the best crime novels have in common is an ability to look beyond the obvious, to reveal the unexpected, to dig beneath the fronts we all wear for the world and discover dark secrets.

There is another reason for checking news media for story ideas. Today there is an appetite amongst readers and, more importantly, publishers, for books that involve the sort of issues that feature in newspapers, on the radio and on television. No longer do crime stories involve upper middle class house parties or Miss Marple-type villages. Single mothers, immigration, juvenile delinquency, ethnic difficulties, tensions involving aged parents, fraud in the work place, equal rights, in fact any of the problems that we all get involved with one way or another can provide valuable background. We will discuss these issues and how they can fire a crime novel a little later.

Exercise

Take a daily newspaper and find a story in it that can start you thinking about a plot. Write down six 'what ifs'. Now look at them, is there sufficient conflict involved to produce suspense? Is there an issue involved? Could you weave a plot around your 'what ifs', or use them to produce further ideas? Could the characters be interesting?

I looked through an issue of a popular daily newspaper after setting this exercise and quickly found a story featuring a lottery winner of millions whose father was separated from the family. He claimed he was denied access to his children, two daughters, and that, though one of them was in touch with him, the lottery winner was not.

We all know what problems money can cause and I began to think about this situation and came up with the following list of 'what ifs':

1. What if some little while after the lottery win is announced, the winner disappears and the police are called in, as it looks as though she could have been abducted?
2. What if the police discover that her father has been seen in the area and the mother says he has been trying to get money out of the girl; he has always been out for the main chance, i.e. an opportunity to make real money for himself?
3. What if when the father is found, he says that he only wanted to get together with his daughter again and she'd been delighted to be reunited with him? He didn't want anything out of her and the break-up of the marriage with her mother was not his fault?
4. What if the girl's boyfriend is discovered to be spending money freely, when before he had nothing, and he says the girl gave it to him to make arrangements for them to go abroad and buy a house in Spain?
5. What if the sister is discovered to have had a violent quarrel with the lottery winner because she wanted to be given part of the winnings to buy a house, so she could settle down with and marry her own boyfriend, and the winner had refused?

6. What if the mother had been overheard also having a violent argument with her daughter because she wanted her to give her husband (the girl's step-father) enough money to start his own restaurant and the girl refused, saying she'd never been able to stand him?

The plot could then have all sorts of possibilities. Perhaps the girl's body could be found. Or maybe she could be discovered being held captive, having been kidnapped in such a way that she didn't know who was responsible, but still refusing to sign away a large portion of her winnings. Maybe the father had been spinning a story and had been responsible, or maybe not. Or maybe the girl disappeared for reasons of her own.

What sort of story will you be comfortable writing?

When considering whether a news story contains an idea that could prove useful for a plot, ask yourself if it would fit into the sort of story you would be comfortable writing.

However horrific the murder or heinous the fraud, or whatever crime you choose, you have to be able to enter into the mind of your villain as well as that of your investigator and the other characters. None of us likes to think that we are capable of any sort of crime, let alone one that is horrific. Nor do most of us believe that our relations and friends and the people we mix with could be either. But all of us are fired to anger, to uncharitable thoughts, to jealousy, and a host of other far from praiseworthy emotions. How far is it from thought to action? The more you can understand the motives that drive people to perpetrate crimes, the stronger and more effective your plot will be.

Let's look at another way of getting ideas for a plot:

Fairy tales – the truth

A well-known fairy tale can give you an idea for a modern story if you look behind the story-line that you are so familiar with. Exactly what was Grandma doing in that bed before the wolf came along? And what sort of a wolf was it? A serial killer wolf? One who had a grudge against grandma? What about the relationship between the wolf and Little Red Riding Hood? Is he a paedophilic wolf? Does he want her to show him what is in her basket? How long before she recognises it's a wolf underneath the disguise?

I went to a workshop on television writing run by Steve Wetton (see his book, *Writing TV Scripts,* published by Studymates, essential reading if you are interested in that area) and he suggested we all use a fairy story to write a scenario. Strong familiarity with the story meant we could concentrate on the technicalities.

My crime writer's mind got working as I looked at Hansel and Gretel, those two little children wooed by the wicked witch into her gingerbread house. What if – those words again – what if Hansel was a bully who had made Gretel accompany him into the wood and this was the latest in a long line of bully-boy tactics? What if Gretel had been burning with hatred against him for the way he behaved towards her? After she and her brother had shoved the witch into the oven, mightn't she have pushed Hansel in as well? Who would know Gretel had done it? She'd be hailed as a heroine for dealing with the witch and everyone would grieve that she hadn't been able to save her brother.

That scenario could be brought up-to-date.

For instance, brother and sister could be in business together. Hansel is the managing director and a bully. Gretel hates the way he treats her but is too ambitious to leave as she knows she could run the company herself; she just needs the right opportunity. The company is threatened with a take-over by a large corporation. The sister masterminds the out-witting of the company but in the moment of triumph, the brother is discovered dead, perhaps in the company factory. It looks like an accident, but is it? Soon an investigation is under way.

Exercise

Take a fairy tale and look at what could lie behind the version we all know so well and see if it could provide the basic framework for a crime novel.

One of the ways to write a crime novel that sells is to have an idea that is really different, one that can grab the reader from the very start. Harlan Coben was a well-regarded American crime writer who had produced a number of books that had sold well, but not sensationally well. Then he wrote *Tell No One*. In it a husband appears to be contacted by the wife he knows is dead. So starts a roller-coaster of a book that keeps you guessing right up until the last page and has more twists and turns in it than Hampton Court maze. It shot Harlan Coben into the top-selling author class, and since then he's produced more equally compelling and twisty books, each with a genuinely different plot.

Ideas like these are not easy to dream up. Robert Goddard, the top-selling English author and a master of involved story lines, says that after he has arrived at what could be seen by others as a satisfyingly complex plot, he looks for an additional twist or two to the story that will take it into new territory.

Remember that any book requires more than one idea. Russell James says, 'Modern plots are more complex than those of yesteryear. To have a detective hero wander through a series of investigative interviews until truth is revealed will not do. You must add more... In American crime fiction the key to a top-selling plot is the *twist* – the succession of twists. Everyone good at the start of the book will have switched to bad before the end; the apparent victim will have become the villain, the dead will be found alive. Whatever expectations the detective and the gullible reader had when the case began will be turned upside down.'

A Small Death in Lisbon by Robert Wilson was awarded the CWA Gold Dagger for fiction. It has a complicated plot which opens with a brief look at the murder of a girl in the present time, then goes back to Berlin during the Second World War and introduces Felsen, a shady industrialist despatched to Portugal by the Nazis to oversee the production of wolfram, essential for the war effort; a task involving corruption, murder and political chicanery. The book then switches between Felsen's subsequent career and the investigation of the girl's murder in present-day Lisbon.

It is a complex novel of greed and corruption that works on many different levels. It is a perfect demonstration of how rich a crime novel can be.

Sub-plots

As well as the main plot, the crime novel needs one or more sub-plots. These should reflect the main plot in some way and they typically involve the main protagonist. Keith Miles points out that they can enrich the texture of a book.

Let's have a look at the Hansel and Gretel plot I outlined above. Gretel is obviously a very disturbed girl. What are her parents like? Could they be driven professionals who have employed a succession of au pairs to look after their children while they work so that the children have grown up without being able to form a loving relationship?

Perhaps Gretel in her role as a businesswoman has a female assistant, let's call her Helen. The assistant might be a single mother having trouble with her teenage son. Alongside the investigation into Hansel's death, there could be a sub-plot involving the disappearance of Helen's son from their holiday home in Cornwall. Once again we have a child who is suffering from parental neglect. Perhaps Gretel can empathise with the son and also appreciate the difficulties the mother is having. As the investigation proceeds, and Gretel has trouble running the company, Helen realises that her job is too stressful and is brought by the agony of not knowing where her son is to realise that she needs to find a job that is less demanding. The sub-plot can be brought into the main plot when her son is at last tracked down and it becomes clear that the boy has some vital information about Hansel's death. Frightened by the implications, he had run away.

Let's look also at the embryonic plot that developed out of the questions I wrote down round the death of Mary, the forty-year old woman. The main action of the plot would revolve around the victim, how she was murdered, who by and why. But during the investigation her adopted daughter could develop a relationship with her birth mother. The loan agent who came to collect his payment may be undergoing a moral crisis that leads him to give up his job by the end of the book. A neighbour could be in an unsatisfactory relationship with her husband and perhaps having an affair with Mary's husband. The investigator may have a neglected partner but by the end of the book has found some way of reconciling their difficulties.

Sub-plots should in some way reflect the theme of the main plot, and should be interesting in themselves but should not deflect too much attention from the main action of your book.

Exercise

Take one of the plots you have developed and plan two or three sub-plots that can work with the main plot.

Using specialised knowledge

Using some interesting specialised knowledge can lift your plot out of the ordinary. Remember Peter Lovesey's item on the joint of meat used to aid the fermentation of cider that inspired his crime novel *Rough Cider*. I saw an item once about an English couple who kept venomous snakes and seven-foot crocodiles at the bottom of their garden. The possibilities for conflict between them and their neighbours are immediately obvious, especially if the crocodile or some of the snakes escape. Had someone released them? Had either the husband or the wife, or maybe an assistant, been careless? Immediately you can see conflict between the couple and their neighbours, and perhaps also between each other. Maybe one half of the couple thinks their partner would make a great meal for the crocodile. Maybe someone else in the village has designs on one of the crocodiles as a novel way of committing murder. But who is the intended victim?

We will examine using specialised backgrounds in more detail in Chapter Six.

So now get started

You may well have had lots of ideas before you started this book. If not, by now your mind should be fizzing with them. I hope you will be getting lots more. If you start doing the exercises suggested in this chapter regularly, you will soon find ideas for crime plots popping up all over the place.

Now it's time to go on to the next stage – deciding what sort of crime novel you are going to write.

Plotting & ideas

 - ➢ Read newspapers for ideas that can produce plots
 - ➢ Start plotting by asking questions
 - ➢ Develop conflict and suspense
 - ➢ Look behind facts for plot possibilities
 - ➢ Use fairy tales for plot ideas
 - ➢ Look for a plot idea that is truly different
 - ➢ Develop sub-plots
 - ➢ Use specialised knowledge.

Choosing An Approach and Dealing With Outlines

After reading this chapter you should be able to sort out your approach to your novel and produce an outline – or decide you are the sort of author that doesn't use one.

Different approaches

Anybody who has read works from a variety of crime authors quickly realises that there are a number of different categories that the books could be slotted into. Some are grittily realistic, others psychologically-involving. There are crime novels that take a gentler path through the murky undergrowth of murder and other illegal activities. Some set their plots in the past, some look at current social issues.

Each of these approaches will appeal to different writers – and readers – and utilise different skills.

Exercise

Make a list of as many different sorts of crime novel as you can think of. Try to use one word categories such as: noir, cosy, etc.

Categories of crime novel

The following categories were used by a bookstore specialising in crime::

- Adventure – Blokeish thriller, war, international politics, espionage
  e.g.: Colin Forbes, Tom Clancy, Paul Eddy

These are fast-moving stories, intent on keeping the reader turning the page. The really successful ones need plausibility of action and depth of characterisation.

- Comic – black humour
  e.g.: Peter Gutteridge, Ruth Dudley Edwards, Janet Evanovich

This is perhaps the most difficult approach of all, it requires plotting skills, excellent characterisation and the ability to sustain an atmosphere that can illuminate the ridiculous and find the comic without losing the thread of the action/plot.

- Hardboiled (sometimes known as 'noir') – scary and/or violent stuff, guns and blood in the Chandler tradition
  e.g.: Walter Moseley with Easy Rawlins, John Connolly, James Lee Burke, some of Val McDermid

The Americans are superb at this; it takes guts and great story-telling abilities to pull it off. If the graphic descriptions of unpleasant developments are to be acceptable, motivation and characterisation need careful realisation – and sensation should never be used merely for effect.

- Historical – set in the past, which can cover any period from earliest times to about the 1960s.
  e.g.: Lindsey Davis, Peter Lovesey, C J Sansom, Andrew Taylor, Steven Saylor, Michael Jecks

There are as many different approaches to the historical crime novel as there are to the contemporary. You need the ability to soak yourself in your chosen era and make it as real to your reader as modern life, whilst still producing all the other crime novel requirements. Many successful historical crime novelists lace their plots with rich period detail that recreates the sights, sounds and smells of their chosen period. Such detail by itself is not enough to make a rewarding book; it has to be accompanied by good plotting and characterisation.

Keith Miles, who has written a number of historical crime novels, advises, 'Do your research thoroughly. The more you investigate the criminal elements in a specific period, the more ideas will be generated. When a story catches your eye, see how you can adapt it – or parts of it – into fiction. Build up a stock of ideas. It may be years before you have the opportunity to develop some of them into a full-length novel but that does not matter. You are learning to gather useful material all the time and that's part of your stock-in-trade.'

Lately more and more serious – what are often called 'literary' – writers are looking at historical settings for complex and extremely well-written crime novels. Barry Unsworth's *Morality Play* is one of these. Though not generally considered to be part of the crime genre, it contains all the elements, and is a marvellous example, of an investigation into a mysterious death. The solution is unexpected, satisfying, and tragic.

- Legal – a crime novel involving the legal system, often the investigation is conducted by a lawyer. There is usually some courtroom drama.
  e.g.: John Grisham, Natasha Cooper

Often this approach can provide interesting insights into the difficulties members of the public find themselves in when caught up in legalities. Lawyers, without being policemen, have a privileged position as far as accessing evidence is concerned. The law pitted against the police can make an interesting conflict. However, complexities of the law must not be allowed to swamp the story. As far as writing these mysteries is concerned, some legal experience is valuable but not essential. The author, though, needs to feel comfortable in this world and be willing to undertake the research that will be required.

- P.I. – Private Eye on the case with optional wisecracking
  e.g.: Val McDermid, Sara Paretsky, Sue Grafton

This approach suits the loner protagonist, the person who is happiest working on their own rather than as part of a team. The PI is usually a quirky character whose personality infuses the book, which can be one of the main attractions for the reader. However, a twisty plot and well-realised characters are also required.

Private Eyes have their own procedures for working on cases. Authors choosing one as their investigator and main protagonist need a knowledge of how they operate, and what can be achieved in an investigation that does not have the resources of the police. First person narration works very well for this type of book, indeed, it could almost be said to be a necessity.

- Police Procedural – The investigation seen from inside the police force.
  e.g.: Michael Collins, Ed McBain, Reginald Hill, Ian Rankin, Simon Kernick, Mark Billingham, Jill McGowan, etc, etc.

These books need a close knowledge of police procedure. In recent years police characters in crime novels, just as in real life, have not all been bolt upright. Corruption, over-zealousness to obtain results, and tension between officers all play their part. Frequently the action will include more than one main protagonist. For further discussion on Police Procedurals, see Chapter Six.

- Psychological
  e.g.: J Wallis Martin, Minette Walters, Phil Lovesey, Denise Mina, Margaret Murphy

These crime novels can utilise the 'amateur detective' or no detective at all. They offer mystery and a good deal of suspense rather than the more familiar investigative procedural. This approach usually leads to a 'one-off' book rather than a series, as it is difficult to use the same character in a number of different psychological mysteries, though Denise Mina has managed it. The books look deep inside the mind of the main characters, and often involve a sinister individual playing upon weaknesses in their victim(s). They can also involve an emotional and mental journey that has to be undergone before the victim can triumph over their assailant. The author requires at least some knowledge of psychology and an acquaintanceship with how the twisted human mind works.

- Traditional – amateur sleuth
  e.g.: Denise Mina, Priscilla Masters, Michelle Spring

This is still a popular approach but is increasingly difficult to make plausible. My books featuring Darina Lise, cordon bleu cook, fall into this category. If I were starting today, I'd take a different approach. With the growth of the importance of forensic examinations in crime investigations (see Chapter Six), the amateur detective has increasing difficulty in solving crimes without access to this information. I overcame it to a certain extent by partnering Darina with a detective, first as boyfriend and then as a husband. (See Chapter Six for further discussion on amateur sleuths.)

These are very broad categories and there are books that defy such arbitrary classification. One such is *A Small Death in Lisbon,* which I referred to in Chapter One. Trying to fit your novel into a particular niche is not the best way to approach writing. You need to concentrate on telling your story in the best way you can, rather than (trying) to decide whether it can be categorised. However, a study of what the market finds acceptable can only help when it comes to writing your book. Seeing what other authors have achieved may provide inspiration or help with deciding your approach. Spending time at the library or amongst the crime section of your local bookshop can be illuminating. And it has to be said that publishers do tend to like books of debut novelists that fit into an established niche.

Discovering what sells

Make friends with your local bookseller and ask which crime books are popular with their customers. Booksellers love books and reading and always seem happy to talk to writers; I've yet to hear of one that minds if the writer has yet to have published a book or not.

Concentrate on looking at first-time authors to see what publishers are currently interested in. Remember that well-established authors have built up a following for their books over years and may be able to continue writing in a way that might not be so welcome from an unknown entrant into the field.

A Sunday newspaper recently submitted typed/printed manuscripts of the openings of two Booker prize-winning novels, from twenty years ago, to twenty publishers and agents. Only one, an agent, wanted to see any more of the manuscripts. The newspaper held that this showed that modern publishers and agents were unable to recognise true writing merit and it may well be that that is the case. However, the literary scene moves on, just as does painting, the film world and every other form of creativity. What was admirable in the past can be admired today, but today's exponents work in a different way.

Exercise

Write down the sort of crime novel you enjoy reading. Make your description as detailed as possible, note down your favourite authors and try to define why exactly it is that you enjoy them.

If you haven't so far read any crime books, start now! Zoe Sharp says she is often amazed at how many people come up to her at literary events and say they are writing a crime novel but don't actually read about crime, or even read much fiction. 'I know some authors who limit their reading while they're actually writing a book, so that they don't pick up someone else's style, but I feel the best way to become a better writer is to read plenty of very well-written books by other people. It's like wanting to be a star footballer, but never watching any of the greats play just in case it influences your style.'

Zoe also suggests that reading 'bad' fiction – if something so subjective can be classified –is valuable too. 'Take it apart. Why doesn't this hold your attention? What about it doesn't work? How can you avoid making the same mistakes in your own work? And what better reason to get on with your novel than because you harbour a sneaking suspicion that you can produce a better book than this!'

The odds are high that you will enjoy writing the sort of book that embodies the same approach that you enjoy reading. And if you haven't been reading crime novels, ask yourself why not. It could be that, if you haven't been interested in reading them, you will not enjoy writing them.

Publishers want authors to be able to produce a number of books that the same readers will enjoy. This means that they will expect you to produce a second novel in the same style as your first. Publishers find it difficult to sell an author that writes a grittily realistic noir novel for their debut and then follows that up with a comfortable, traditional type of story. If readers have enjoyed the first book, they are going to expect the next to offer the same sort of experience.

Think of the novels of Dick Francis. When you pick up one of his books, you have a very good idea of what awaits you. Even when the background isn't horse racing, the elements of a Francis novel are the same. It will be written in the first person by a morally driven, intelligent, humane investigator; there will be an emphasis on action as well as mystery (which is sometimes solved quite early on); interesting characters who are often morally flawed; and an easy style that carries you along. Once a Dick Francis novel has been started, it is very difficult to put down. These are all very attractive qualities that have ensured a vast following for each book as soon as it is published.

Your sort of crime novel

What sort of book will you be happy writing?

If you find twisted personalities interesting and challenging and enjoy trying to get inside the minds of people who can commit horrific crimes, both the hardboiled/noir and the psychological approaches could be successful ones for you.

If, though, you shrink from reading very gory scenes and do not enjoy plots involving violent characters, you will want to steer clear of the noir approach.

Do you enjoy making life as comfortable as possible and like a feel-good factor in the books you read? In that case, you will probably be happiest with what is called the 'cosy' type of crime novel. This is usually a traditional approach involving an amateur detective or someone with an official interest that is not that of a police officer, which focuses on interesting characters rather than action-packed events.

Perhaps you love watching police dramas on television. You may have some experience of police work. You may enjoy forensic detail and the minutiae of an official investigation. If so, the police procedural style may well work for you.

Beware, though, of stereotyping your approach. Your book has to be one that you really want to write and if it doesn't fit into an accepted pattern, it may be that what you write is so fresh and original, it will find a publisher. Jake Arnott's *The Long Firm* combined a number of different approaches. It is both hardboiled and psychological. It is told in three parts, each taking the story forward a number of years and each told from a very different viewpoint from the previous one. It starts in the fifties and brilliantly recaptures the gangland London of the period. It proved so successful that it was subsequently made into a critically acclaimed television serial.

Exercise

Take a plot that you have been working on that interests you. What sort of crime novel do you think it could work as? Think carefully about the general atmosphere of your plot and the sort of characters it involves. Write out a brief synopsis in the style of maybe one or two of the different approaches discussed in this chapter. Which would suit it best? Is it the first of a series featuring some sort of investigator, perhaps a police procedural? Is it a hardboiled, noir novel with lots of gritty, realistic detail? Or an action-packed story in the Dick Francis mode? Perhaps it should be a traditional mystery that relies on interesting characters and a twisty plot rather than gory action.

After doing this exercise, you may well find that you have happily fitted your embryonic plot into a format that offers possibilities for the sort of book you would like to write. You could be itching to start, have all sorts of ideas that you can see how to put into action – which is wonderful. And I hope you find the rest of this book helpful in writing a successful crime novel.

Perhaps, though, you have lots of ideas but, even after thinking hard around the categories we have discussed, do not think that they will fit into a basic format. Maybe you feel your book would be far too individual to be typed in this way. If so, try and remember two things. The first is that, even if a book seems to fit into a category, if it is at all successful, it will have a particular uniqueness, an identity of its own, that will make it stand out from others which booksellers see as following the same approach. After all, even a three-piece suit is capable of many different looks, and so is a ball gown.

The second point to remember is that you may well write a book that can't easily be summed up as fitting into any category, but it still has to be sold in order to reach readers. Booksellers and publishers today want to be able to divide books and bookshelves into easily defined areas. They have developed an approach that can be summed up as: 'If you like the books of such and such a writer, you will enjoy this one too.' A new writer who introduces a forensic pathologist as their protagonist is hailed as the new Patricia Cornwell. The Canadian writer, Kathy Reichs, used to be so bracketed; now, many books later, she has achieved her own status. If, therefore, your book breaks out into a brave new path, it has to be so outstandingly good a publisher has to find a way to persuade booksellers it should be allocated a special place on their shelves.

It is not impossible to defy categorisation, I'm just pointing out that it's difficult and that breaking into the publishing world is a hard task at the best of times.

It can't be said often enough, though, that every book is a unique product. It has to arise out of an author's imagination and grow organically in that author's mind. Its characters have to have lives of their own. Readers should feel they know them as well as they know the people they regularly mix with in real life. We will come to characterisation in the next chapter. First, though, I want to look at outlines.

Outlines – are they needed?

Writers are often asked whether they prepare a detailed outline before writing a book and there are many different answers.

Some authors prepare elaborate chapter breakdowns with every character and development in their story fully worked out. Others start with a basic idea and the opening to their book, then sit down and write as though they are the reader, discovering the story as they go along. Still others do an outline that varies in complexity from a couple of pages to the fully worked out model mentioned above. There is no right or wrong way, only what works for you.

There are, as in so many other areas of life, advantages and disadvantages in all these different approaches.

Advantages of an outline

Particularly with crime novels, it is important to know that you have a plot that is going to work, that means it should have a beginning, which introduces the mystery; a middle, which presents the meat of the investigation; and an ending, where all is revealed. Writing an outline ensures that all the pieces of the action and the motivations for the characters will fit together, that the plot, in fact, works.

An outline is a route map for the writing of the book. It can show how everything in your plot fits together: the characters, their motivation, the crime, the investigation, and the denouement. It can save you a great deal of time as, without it, you may find that you have to backtrack in order to set up a development you had not foreseen.

Writers, though, vary in their attitudes to outlines.

Peter Lovesey holds that, for him, 'planning is the key to writing a good crime novel. My output of words is abysmally low, about 200 per day, so I can't afford to rewrite. If I had to work in drafts I'd never finish.' After plotting the story in his head and jotting down important twists and surprises, essential ingredients in a good mystery, he writes a ten to twelve page synopsis of the plot in detail. His story outline takes a couple of months and will contain all the major events, twists, and surprises. He'll know the locations and the characters pretty well at this stage. 'With all those decisions made I can then get to the enjoyable part of putting down the words in ways that please me – and please the reader, I hope.'

Another writer for whom they are essential is Michael Jecks. 'It is very important that a story has a natural flow. A reader must want to continue with it, and for that to happen there must be a steadiness to the tale. I write up all the scenes on enormous post-it notes, which are three feet by two, roughly. It takes me about three of these to outline a four hundred page novel. Every scene is on there, so I can gauge whether one character has too much of the book to himself. Also I can make sure that there is a scene depicting action or tension fairly regularly, and I can see that, for example, all suspects have been questioned! If you can't get hold of these huge post-it notes, do what I used to do: I tore old manuscripts and note-papers into four strips and used blu-tack to stick them to the wall. This has the added benefit that I could lift scenes and push them further up the storyline, or pull them back earlier without scribbling!' He adds that it had the disadvantage that on one occasion it pulled the paint off the wall.

An outline can also help you decide in which direction you are going to point the reader (never the right one as far as solving the mystery is concerned), and at what stage you are going to alter that direction so that they suspect a different character (we will go into this in more detail later).

For me an outline gives a sense of security. It's like a lifeline. You have a comfortable feeling that the plot works, that a basic structure is in place. This means that you now can work on telling the story in the most effective way possible, rather than worrying about time and method of death and whether you've got the suspects in the right places.

Disadvantages of an outline

The main disadvantage of an outline is that it can interfere with your book growing organically.

Ann Granger never writes a synopsis or outline. 'I know where I'm starting and where I want to end up, but how I'm going to get there I have no idea until I start writing. I need to put words on paper, or up on the screen, then the ideas come and the whole project grows, a little like Topsy. I write in a series of drafts. My latest book took three drafts and one of my earlier ones, *Shades of Murder,* went through seven drafts . . . I feel a book is a living thing. You can't just box it in any more than you can box in a wild creature. You just hope you'll be able to tame it and make it do what you want it to. That sounds a bit fanciful but I don't quite know how to put it another way. I think of Michelangelo or some other sculptor wrestling with a lump of marble and trusting that eventually he'll have a finished piece of work; I just keep chipping away at my text.'

There is no doubt that, however detailed an outline you prepare, it is only when writing the book itself that you really get inside your characters. Then you may have prepared a detailed outline but come to a point in the story when you realise that the path you have outlined is not the road your characters want to travel. You have probably heard writers speak of 'characters taking over the plot'. This can happen when the people you have created seem to take on a life of their own and they tell you, rather like rebellious children, they must do things their way, not yours.

If you find this happening, don't fight it. Look again at your outline and consider how it should be changed. If you force the lifelike characters you have created to behave in a way that no longer is realistic, the book will lack a basic truth and readers will almost certainly feel dissatisfied.

There may be other reasons to adjust or even abandon your outline. As you write your book, unexpected possibilities may present themselves. New ideas often arrive and provide a fresh inspiration. You may find that when writing your story in detail, some part of your plot doesn't work. Maybe you overlooked something vital. You may even find you have written the same character in two different places at same time, not too difficult if you have a complicated structure told from different points of view.

Another disadvantage of a detailed outline is that it may tempt you to 'surface write'. That is, instead of digging down and examining exactly what is going on with your characters and your plot, you merely flesh out the skeleton you have created. It's only when skeletons have life breathed into them that they become interesting. However carefully you consider an outline, and however elaborately you have sketched it, the story will not come alive until you actually sit down and write it. Concentrate too closely on an outline and you may miss something seething below your clever plot which could bring it into vivid life, and make it a bestseller.

An outline should be an aid, not a crutch. It should not make you write as though you are painting by numbers.

Forms of outline

There are various forms of outline, and they include:

> A simple outline summarises the plot and the characters and can run from one to several pages. It allows for a great deal of organic growth in writing the book but may fail to identify tricky areas that have been skated over because of your excitement with the power of your plot.

> A more detailed outline will trace the events and characters in your book from the beginning to the end. This should sort out whether there are any major holes in your plot, and/or poor motivation on the part of your characters, while still allowing for development as you write. However, it may not be able to give a proper shape to the telling of your story; it may not show where climaxes come, where the pace has to quicken, even where scenes will be set or how they can be contrasted with each other.

> A chapter breakdown is what it says: an account of what will go into each chapter from start to finish.

This again can be more or less elaborate, from a short list of plot points to a detailed account of each scene, where it is set, what it contains and how it contributes to character development, etc, etc. A good chapter breakdown can create the atmosphere and shape of a book as well as work out all plot points.

There are writers who work out such a detailed chapter-by-chapter breakdown that they are able to write scenes out of order, knowing that they will fit into the story as a whole. But, as noted above, such detail can also prevent a writer getting right inside the story and letting it itself dictate what will happen. The author who uses such an approach has to be able to envisage the whole development of the story, and exactly how the characters will interact and the plot unfold.

When I plan a book, I first of all write out a brief synopsis of the plot that gives the mechanics behind the story, what could be called the nuts and bolts. Then I write detailed notes on each of the characters. Sometimes this gives me more ideas for the plot that will mean the outline will need tweaking and adjusting. This is an exciting stage when anything seems possible.

After making the character notes, I go back to my outline and do a lot of thinking. Gradually I expand the detail, bring in some scenes, maybe some sub-plots – which will mean more character notes. Nothing at this stage seems set in stone, I feel free to add and subtract plot points, scenes and characters, as I try to give shape to the book.

During this process, the book takes on a momentum of its own and there comes a stage when I know I have to leave outlining and start writing – in fact I can't wait to start writing.

My outlines, though, however detailed they might be, always have one big omission. They never have an ending. I know who has done the murder (so far I have always dealt in murder), I know who the victim or victims will be. I have notes on the characters and what motivates them. I have ideas for sub-plots and for how the investigation will proceed – but when it comes to the denouement, there is a blank.

When I first started writing books, this lack of an ending worried me. I would spend a considerable amount of time trying to work out how I was going to reveal the murderer and bring the story to an end. Finally I would give up and, because the book was panting to be written, I'd start on it anyway. Always by the time the denouement was reached, I knew what had to happen. It didn't always come right with the first draft but there would be a rough shape that I could refine as I worked through the book a second time.

Writing a book is an organic process, and for many authors much of the growth occurs not in an outline but in the actual business of putting the words together that form the book rather than a précis of it. I mentioned earlier that an outline could be a route map. Maps enable you to choose where you want to go and how to get there, but these decisions can be altered if more interesting options turn up on the journey.

Exercise

Take your murder plot and chosen approach and outline the first three chapters, giving details of events and characters.

I went back to the story of forty-year old Mary discovered battered to death in her home. After a little thought I decided that, for this sort of story, a traditional approach would work well, although I did wonder whether I would make it a police procedural. However, I decided that someone involved with Mary could make a more interesting viewpoint than a detective.

Chapter One: Jane Wilson arrives to see her sister, Mary Banks. Jane is a loss adjuster for an insurance company and has been sent to assess the damage a flood has done to a nearby house. Finishing earlier than she expected, she decides to see if Mary is home as she is worried about her sister. She arrives at the house just after the neighbour discovers Mary's battered body. Overcome with shock, Jane discovers that the neighbour hasn't called the police yet and finds her behaviour suspicious. Jane takes charge and phones a doctor and the police. The neighbour tells Jane that Mary's daughter has left home. Also that Mary's husband left her two months ago, a fact Jane was unaware of. Looking through her sister's papers before the police arrive, she finds a letter from the birth mother of Mary's adopted daughter, Helen. In it, Irene Thompson, the birth mother, says it is no use Mary trying to prevent Helen from living with her and that if she continues to threaten Irene, it will be the worse for her. Jane, deeply shocked and puzzled, pockets the letter as the police arrive on the scene.

Chapter Two: Jane meets the detective in charge of the case, Ken Lane. He is furious that she has started to go through her sister's desk before his arrival. In fact, it quickly becomes clear that he is suspicious of her presence on the scene as she betrays how little she knows of her sister's life and circumstances. Jane does not tell him about the letter from Irene Thompson. Jane is heartbroken at her sister's death and the realisation of how far she and her sister, who had once been so close, have drifted apart. Jane has a broken marriage behind her, as her husband couldn't cope with a wife who earned more than he did and was so often away from home. She decides that if she is the detective's chief suspect, she will do all she can to find out who actually did murder her sister.

Chapter Three: The following day, Jane, now staying in a local hotel, visits Irene Thompson, discovers she is a widow, and is taken aback to find out how wealthy and sophisticated she is. Helen is out at college. Irene laughs off the letter but does not seem distressed at Mary's death. She tells Jane that Mary could not offer Helen all the advantages she can and now there is nothing to prevent the two of them forming a close relationship. Helen already loves her, Irene says. She refuses to let Jane tell Helen of Mary's death but agrees to let the girl know where Jane is staying.

Arriving back, depressed, at her hotel, Jane is dismayed to find a message from her boss telling her she must return immediately, she cannot be allowed to take the time off she wants so she can find out how her sister was murdered.

These three chapter outlines have been developed from the quick questions I put down in response to that early exercise. You can see how some of the original ideas are still there but that others have been modified. New characters have arrived and the investigation has started.

Since doing the chapter outline above, I've had other ideas. It might add resonance to the story if I make Jane a woman who has conquered alcoholism, an addiction which could have contributed to the failure of her marriage. Perhaps she tried to help Mary conquer her gambling addiction and Mary reacted by cutting herself off from Jane. Then Jane could be fired from her firm for refusing to return to her work. As she trawls through the murk of Mary's life, tries to outwit Ken Lane, the detective, and to deal with the fall-out in her own life, she could face the temptation of turning to drink for comfort.

Before I can take the story much further, though, I need to take a good look at a possible setting and get to know my characters. Also, I need to consider whether I want to look at the problems of addiction as a background to the story.

Settings and issues are the subjects of the next chapter.

Approaches & outlines

➢ Study recently published crime novels for types of approach
➢ Decide what sort of novel you enjoy reading – that is most likely to be the sort of novel you will be comfortable writing
➢ Suit your approach to your plot
➢ Make sure your story is not a stereotype
➢ Decide what sort of outline will be helpful then write one for the first three chapters of a plot

3 Settings and Issues

Settings

There are writers for whom books start with a location. P D James has said that places play a major part in her books. Turn to any one of them and you will find that the story revolves around a specific place. A dark tower, a London church, a nuclear power station, they have all been central to one of her stories. Each setting is vividly described and its atmosphere permeates the plot.

Val McDermid's wonderful book *A Place of Execution* is steeped in its Peak District location. It is impossible to imagine the story taking place anywhere else.

Marjorie Allingham's classic book *The Tiger in the Smoke*, first published in 1952, uses the background of London and its winter fog to create an atmosphere both menacing and mysterious. Here is a flavour:

> The fog was like a saffron blanket soaked in ice-water. It had hung over London all day and at last was beginning to descend. The sky was yellow as a duster and the rest was a granular black, overprinted in grey and lightened by occasional slivers of bright fish colour as a policeman turned in his wet cape.
>
> Already the traffic was at an irritable crawl. By dusk it would be stationary. To the west the Park dripped wretchedly and to the north the great railway terminus slammed and banged and exploded hollowly about its affairs. Between lay winding miles of butter-coloured stucco in every conceivable state of repair.

Even though today, thanks to the Clean Air Act, we no longer experience the pea-souper winter fogs that could bring London traffic to a standstill and lethally invade fragile lungs, we can conjure up their effect through this remarkable book.

John D MacDonald set his *Travis McGee* stories on the Florida waterside. He wrote these compelling tales while

Florida was being developed into the commercial and tourist big-time it is now. The contrast between the casual beach life with its boat-bums, and the political and business corruption ballooning all around, provided him with a rich cast of characters and an unending series of criminal activities for the layabout, womanising, cynical but highly principled yachtsman, Travis McGee.

Ian Rankin sets his highly successful *Rebus* stories in Edinburgh, revealing the seedy side of a city most see as upper class and full of period charm.

Reginald Hill sets his equally successful series of *Dalziel and Pascoe* crime novels in mid-Yorkshire, which offers him both beautiful landscape and a variety of urban locations.

Each of these writers, and I could have named many more, makes their chosen locations a central feature of their books.

They do not always choose the same locations. Val McDermid set *The Mermaids Singing,* the first of her hardboiled series featuring the psychological profiler Tony Hill and the detective Carol Jordan, in Manchester, an urban landscape she knows well from her days as a news editor there. This knowledge anchors the sensational aspects of the book in grim reality.

Even when writing a series around a main character or characters, authors can vary their settings. With considerable ingenuity, P D James sends her high-ranking detective, Adam Dalgleish, into a variety of locations. Reginald Hill has an enviable facility to vary the settings of many of his *Dalziel and Pascoe* novels and Ian Rankin sends *Rebus* to places outside of Edinburgh.

Peter N Walker (Nicholas Rhea) says, 'Because I was brought up in, and now live on the edge, of the North York Moors (not the dales), I make good use of that picturesque area in my novels.' He adds that writers can fictionalise the locations of their novels. 'One popular device is to use a real town, village or area but give it a fictitious identity. This allows the author to add or delete features as required, and it is possible to create a fictitious location within a real area – for example my Heartbeat village of Aidensfield lies somewhere between the real towns of Whitby, Pickering,

Malton and Scarborough. Indeed, some readers still believe it is a real village and spend time looking for it!'

Andrew Taylor has written a series of excellent historical crime novels recreating the atmosphere of a fifties fictional small town on the border between England and Wales north of Bristol, more or less where Monmouth is, which he has called Lydmouth.

Uses of settings

Settings have more to contribute to a story than scenic qualities. Conflict, so essential to the fiction writer, can arise out of a location. People have taken a gun to their neighbours because of a long-running argument over a hedge or a boundary.

Where they live can affect people's behaviour. Life in the big city, to use an obvious example, is not the same as life in the country. If you want to write realistic novels about organised crime, you must almost always look to a big city location such as, for instance, Manchester or London. If it is to be a story involving the effects that the stresses and strains of modern life can have on a character(s), the natural place to set such stories is in a city.

Country life is slower than city life; there nature tends to be more important than technology. Bad weather in the country has much more of an impact on those living there than in a town, where the main nuisances of rain are increased traffic, lack of available taxis, and the necessity for an umbrella. And the absence of rain in town is generally looked on as a blessing; in the country it can be a serious disadvantage to farmers and gardeners.

Community life features more in the country than in towns. In villages, people have to associate with a much wider range of characters than in towns. Social life can often revolve around the village hall and group activities. Next-door neighbours can offer a variety of backgrounds, even if they are sometimes a considerable distance away. This in itself can offer rich possibilities for conflict. Agatha Christie understood this; look at her *Miss Marple* novels.

In urban settings, though, like tends to mix with like. This does not mean that there is less opportunity for conflict but that different influences affect them, such as tensions with ethnic communities, more crime, and the pressure of people living close together.

Geography can play a part in more ways than simply the country versus town dichotomy. The atmosphere amongst northern communities, for instance, is different from those in the south of Britain. The Welsh have their own slant on life, as have the Irish. Small country towns are very different from large urban conurbations where the atmosphere can change from area to area within the shortest of distances.

Choosing a setting

If you are considering embarking on a series of crime novels, you should choose a background capable of sustaining the discovery of a number of bodies.

Colin Dexter sets his famous series of crime novels featuring *Inspector Morse* in Oxford. This is a location offering conflicts amongst academics, who can nurse grudges in a spectacular fashion, as well as conflicts between 'town and gown'. It also has a rich commercial and cultural life together with a country life-style on its doorstep. Morse can find himself investigating crimes involving any of these. The Morse novels raised Oxford's murder rate sensationally, but this did not seem out of character to the readers of the novels.

Exercise

Choose a location as background for a crime series and write a paragraph explaining its potential. Then write a description of a scene that brings it to life for your reader.

To go beside the example quoted above from Marjorie Alligham's *Tiger In The Smoke*, here is the beginning of Val McDermid's *The Last Temptation*, a hardboiled novel that takes the character *Carol Jordan* into Europe:

Blue is one colour the Danube never manages. Slate grey, muddy brown, dirty rust, sweat-stained khaki; all of these and most of the intermediate shades sabotage the dreams of any romantic who stands on her banks. Occasionally, where boats gather, she achieves a kind of oily radiance as the sun shimmers on a skin of spilled fuel, turning the river the iridescent hues of a pigeon's throat. On a dark night when clouds obscure the stars, she's as black as the Styx. But there, in central Europe at the turning of the new millennium, it cost rather more than a penny to pay the ferryman.

The passage sets the atmosphere of the story, one of corruption, deceit and criminality in which the Danube is a major character. There's only one tiny suggestion that beauty and romance could be a part of the great river and even that is compromised: 'she achieves a kind of oily radiance as the sun shimmers on a skin of spilled fuel, turning the river the iridescent hues of a pigeon's throat'.

The better you know your background, the easier it is to incorporate its spirit and atmosphere into your story and to find the unique qualities that will capture the reader. Practise looking around your own environment: what is its atmosphere? How do people react to living there? How would you describe its unique qualities? What details would you choose to capture or highlight those qualities? Could it form the background to a crime scene?

If you travel around the country or abroad, look at where you visit, write descriptions, capture the atmosphere and the essence of where you are. It will not only hone your skills at bringing scenes to life for a reader, it may also provide you with locations.

I set a book, *Death A La Provençale,* in the south of France, where my husband and I had a habit of spending two or three weeks every spring. It's a fascinating area, the over-crowded coast contrasting with the land behind, where ancient villages perch on high hills, deep gorges wind through wooded hills and lakes are surrounded with forests. Everywhere one looks, there are olive groves. We used to visit one of the mills and buy freshly pressed oil. For the book I used several different locations; some were actual, others were imaginary but based on places we had visited, and the story took a look at the life led by foreigners, including the British, down on the Riviera. The making of virgin olive oil played a major part in the book, its natural goodness a contrast to the sophistication and pursuit of the good life of many of the characters.

P D James set her novel *Original Sin* in a private publishing house set on the banks of the Thames. At the start of the book a temporary secretary arrives for an interview. Here is the description of the setting as she sees it for the first time:

> *She found herself on a wide forecourt of gleaming marble bounded by a low railing in delicate wrought iron with at each corner a glass globe supported by entwined dolphins in bronze. From a gap in the middle of the railing a flight of steps led down to the river. She could hear its rhythmic slap against the stone. She walked slowly towards it in a trance of wonder as if she had never seen it before. It shimmered before her, a wide expanse of heaving sun-speckled water which, as she watched, was flicked by the strengthening breeze into a million small waves like a restless inland sea, and then, as the breeze dropped, mysteriously subsided into shining smoothness. And, turning, she saw for the first time the towering wonder of Innocent House, four storeys of coloured marble and golden stone which, as the light changed, seemed subtly to change colour, brightening, then shading to a deeper gold. The great curved arch of the main entrance was flanked by narrow arched windows and above it were two storeys with wide balconies of carved stone fronting a row of slender marble pillars rising to trefoil arches. The high arched windows and marble columns extended to a final storey under the parapet of a low roof. She knew none of the architectural details but she had seen houses like this before on a boisterous ill-conducted school trip to Venice when she was thirteen . . . looking up at the marvel of Innocent House, she felt a belated response to that earlier experience, a mixture of awe and joy which surprised and a little frightened her.*

As in all of P D James's novels, the atmosphere of the setting winds its way through the story and this description makes clear the spell of Innocent House and its location on the banks of London's river.

Issues

A setting can provide a powerful thrust to a plot but it is not the only way into a book.

Val McDermid has said that crime writing is 'the light we shine on the society we live in'. Ian Rankin echoes this: 'right now crime writers around the world are confronting society's deepest problems, worries and uncertainties in a way the "literary" novel sometimes avoids'. Alex Gray says: 'The crime writer asks himself "Why?" when such events as the Soham tragedy (when two small girls were murdered by someone they knew and trusted) takes place. Perhaps the writer wants to make sense of such ghastliness and begins to create a story that provides some feeling of closure.'

These issues are fertile fields for crime writers. 'Societies' deepest problems' involve high emotions: guilt, despair, greed, corruption, innocence betrayed, desperation of all kinds. Conflict is everywhere.

Here's Keith Miles' view, 'Because of its nature, a crime novel can accommodate a vast range of themes. This does not mean that every book must carry a stark message but a strong, underlying theme can bring a novel into focus. If you choose to explore, for instance, immigration issues or political corruption or the defects of a particular legal system, you will be able to say something a little more profound than that Crime Doesn't Pay.'

Organised crime has already been mentioned. Publishers tend to be wary of plots that involve drug dealings but less so of novels that deal with the battle between police and gangland – if a detailed knowledge of the background can be demonstrated. I've already mentioned Simon Kernick and Mark Billingham as successful practitioners in this field.

Conflicts amongst ethnic communities is a comparatively new area that can yield complex and involving crime plots. Lesley Horton's first novel, *Snares of Guilt* is a police procedural that investigates a murder involving an Asian community and focuses on Sikh/Muslim prejudices and tensions. The author increases the difficulties faced by the investigating team by including an Asian on it who has to cope with his own prejudices when assessing evidence and evaluating witnesses.

Garnethill by Denise Mina, set in Glasgow, is a psychological crime story as well as a compelling investigation into murder. The heroine is emerging from the mental difficulties involved in coming to terms with the childhood abuse she suffered from her father, when she discovers in her apartment the murdered body of her psychiatrist lover.

Garnethill won the CWA Creasey Dagger for best first crime novel by a debut author. Denise Mina then took her main character down to London, successfully involving her in more murder and psychological problems.

Minette Walters won the CWA Gold Dagger for her book *Fox Evil*. Set in a Dorset village, the plot combines a community threatened by travellers, with the mystery surrounding the death of a wealthy landowner's elderly wife. The landowner then becomes the victim of a relentless campaign of suspicion. As well as digging deep into the characters and their relationships, the book asks questions about who are outsiders.

Exercise

Take a look through a popular newspaper and choose a story that involves an issue you are particularly interested in. Use it as the basis for working out a crime plot. NB: Use the story only as a starting point; as the source of ideas rather than as a story-frame.

For instance: We could look at the story that broke after Hurricane Katrina devastated New Orleans. The chief of FEMA, the federal emergency management agency, received accusations of inefficiency and an inadequate response to the disaster situation. Publication of emails between the chief and other members of his bureau suggested he had completely failed to comprehend the seriousness of the situation.

There will be, I am sure, thriller and mystery books written featuring Hurricane Katrina and New Orleans but, unless you are very familiar with the American scene and that situation in particular, I would not suggest it as a viable subject for a first crime book. However, if we take the basic situation, a natural disaster, poor official response, and the perceived ineptitude of one authority figure in particular, plus what on the surface seems an uncaring official attitude, then we can transfer that scenario to the UK, or anywhere else for that matter. Floods in various parts of the UK are common and are occasionally major disasters. What if an official who was revealed as incompetent and uncaring in the disaster response was later found murdered?

A number of different approaches could be used. There is the one that could centre on official corruption and local politics. Another one could feature an in-depth look at the flood situation, man against nature, and some personal tragedy that resulted from the disaster. Either book might focus on the flood, its origins, the methods used, or not used, to prevent damage, and the resultant fall out. There would be plenty of scope for conflict between characters, and the investigation into the murder might be conducted by the police, or involve a private person who did not believe whatever the official story was. In both cases, the actual murderer might have had a very different motive from that originally assumed, that it had been a vengeance killing by a disaster victim, and the groundwork for that would have to be threaded through the book.

Once you start looking at news stories in this way, a trawl through the paper on most days can extract possibilities for a crime scenario. The secret is to look behind the obvious and winkle out the personal conflicts that can be identified behind the bare details. The woman arrested for setting up a paid killer to remove her husband, for instance. What is the back-story for both the husband and the wife? Is either of them the person they are commonly assumed to be? Maybe the husband, on the surface an upright citizen, is actually involved with the underworld. Does the wife have something to hide? How does one find a contract killer? What is the evidence for arresting the wife? Could she have been framed? If so, by whom and for what reason? What are the other characters involved – or, more importantly for a crime writer, what characters can you imagine might be involved?

Exercise

Take another story from a newspaper and, using it as a starting point, see what sort of crime plot you can put together. Remember that it doesn't matter how far you stray from the original.

If you practise doing this exercise regularly, you will soon begin to recognise what sort of plot attracts you and how you can put odd facts and issues together to form a crime story. Concentrate on the characters involved, how they interact, what the possibilities for conflict are, what their back-stories could be. Try to imagine how the basic ideas could be developed into a full-blown plot.

Martin Edward's books all have themes. 'Sometimes they reflect the culprit's motivation. For example, fear of loneliness in *All the Lonely People,* the importance of past memories in '*I Remember You*'. In my Lake District mystery series, the unifying theme is the clash of civilisations in Great Britain – increasing urban incursions into traditional rural ways of life. *Take My Breath Away* incorporated a perspective on modern politics and the PR machine.'

Issues can be buried or ignored

If talk about issues and dealing with the evils of society gets you worried, do not despair. There are very successful crime writers who concentrate on more traditional approaches. This is not to say they ignore social issues, an almost impossible task today, but that they treat them with a light hand and deliver entertaining books that involve the reader in intriguing mysteries. Social issues are there but rarely the main theme of the plot. What holds the attention, as with every other kind of crime novel, are believable characters, engrossing mysteries, well worked out plots, and a style of writing that commands the reader's attention.

John Malcolm says, 'I think that there are two approaches to writing crime fiction. One is to treat the horrors of murder, crime and its social origins seriously. The other is to see them as an opportunity for entertainment, adventure and even humour. The second approach, which has a very long history, is the one that appeals to me. It still allows for social comment and the chill of reality, as a mystery is unravelled. It also allows for parody without pretension.'

Issues can be dealt with satirically, with a very light hand, as Ruth Dudley Edwards does with her series of novels, each of which looks at a different area of the British establishment. They are ironic, very funny and also extremely skilful crime novels. As Ruth says, 'Just because it's funny doesn't mean it isn't serious.' She adds this advice, 'If you want to write a comic novel, don't force jokes. If it doesn't make you laugh, it probably won't work for anyone else either.'

Most writers would agree today that is essential to characterisation compelling a successful crime novel, and that is what we are going to look at next.

Settings & issues

> Study how a setting can provide the inspiration and atmosphere for a successful crime novel
> Write descriptions of places you visit that identify atmosphere and character
> Examine where you live and identify its character
> Identify how different places can affect the lives of those who live and work there
> Look at current issues that affect our society and assess how they can provide conflict and plot ingredients for a crime novel

4 Characterisation and Motivation

Any novel is only as successful as its characters and that includes crime novels. The people on your page have to be as vivid and rooted in the real world as the people you meet in your daily life. That goes for historical characters as well. Human nature does not change and motives for murder, as everything else, in Medieval England are much the same as those in the early twenty-first century. The world in which your characters move may well be different from the one in which you live, but their essential nature has not greatly altered.

Characters in a crime novel must, then, be as believable to the reader as their friends, neighbours, or colleagues. Alex Gray says: 'Why a character acts in a certain way is much more pertinent to a crime novel than to any other type of fiction.'

The writer of crime novels, though, has to remember that they are writing a mystery. Characters often need to present a devious front to the world. The simple girl who seems at first sight to be an innocent can, in fact, be a clever, remorseless manipulator of people. It won't necessarily mean she is also a murderer but a gradual revelation of her true character will certainly raise questions in the reader's as well as the investigator's mind.

Plots should be what is known as 'character driven'. That is to say, it is what sort of people your characters are that determines what happens in your plot rather than events. What motivates your characters will decide whether the plot is believable or not. A really twisty plot development may look very clever at first sight but it will only work if the reader believes in the characters and the way they behave. Ann Granger advises, 'Get good characters and you're half way there. A plot on its own is interesting to the extent that reading a newspaper is interesting. You need characters that readers can feel they know.'

Exercise

Take some sort of celebrity, maybe a model or a politician, say, or a sports person, or someone who has suddenly come to prominence through a particular circumstance, all of them fictional of course, and give them a secret life. Describe how they come over on the surface, then go behind the public face and outline how they might actually be. Then dream up a situation in which they reveal their true character.

For instance, you might take someone who has rescued a small child from some disaster and found instant fame. He, let's call him Paul, comes over as a modest, hardworking man with a self-deprecating sense of humour, a happy home life, a wife of twenty years, two teenage children, and a middle-management job. The media embrace him as a people's hero. In fact, Paul is actually a bitter and twisted man who has grown increasingly resentful of the fact that life seems to have passed him by. He is no longer attracted to his wife, his children are difficult, and his job uninteresting. He is aware of time passing by and is desperate to break out of the confines of his boring life before it is too late. Paul is therefore planning to defraud the company he works for of a large sum of money, and to make a new life for himself on the other side of the world.

On an evening out funded by a local newspaper to celebrate the successful rescue of the child, Paul, the seemingly quiet and modest man, and his family are plied with too much alcohol. His children become belligerent when he says they shouldn't have anything more to drink and he explodes, telling them he can't put up with their behaviour. When his wife objects, he includes her in his unpleasant attack and says that things are going to change.

The character outlined above may, in fact, turn out to have nothing to do with murder. If, though, the murder victim turns out to be someone in his firm who may or may not have discovered his fraud, Paul will have a very good motive for murder and the police or the investigator will have been alerted to the fact that he is not what he seems.

Another suggestion:

Alice is a government minister. She has risen to her political height from a deprived background. She has a supportive husband who remains in the background, and three children, mostly looked after by a nanny, although Alice is constantly being quoted on the importance of quality time with them. She is a sparkling personality who engages everyone who meets her.

In fact Alice is hiding a secret that she is terrified is going to catch up with her. Before going up to Oxford, she had a gap year during which she travelled round the world, working her passage in various ways, not all of them legal. In Thailand she very briefly became a drugs carrier, persuaded by the money to take drugs to England, after which she returned to Thailand to repeat the operation. A girl she is friendly with is similarly employed and is caught and imprisoned. Alice narrowly escaped the same fate. Since returning to England, she has been a model citizen. Few people realise that ambition rules her life and that she can be ruthless.

Alice's imprisoned colleague is finally released. Because her incarceration was widely reported and it was followed by a programme of constant appeals for her return to the UK to complete her sentence, the media rush to interview her. They report her bitterness with an unnamed person she thought was a friend but who she blames for her imprisonment. She states that she intends to make that person's life a misery. Almost immediately she is murdered.

At this stage there is no known connection with Alice. However, she reveals something of her true nature when her teenage son is caught in a drugs trap by a tabloid newspaper and is arrested. Alice's husband is in hospital but instead of hurrying to help her son, Alice insists on going ahead with what she considers to be an important speech. Much of the media is shocked by her lack of maternal concern. The outward face has revealed flaws.

Again, Alice may or may not be the murderer, but when some enterprising journalist uncovers the fact that she was in Thailand at exactly the same time as the imprisoned girl, and unearths someone who knows there was a connection between them, more and more questions are asked.

It isn't enough, though, to dream up a character who isn't what they seem, you must understand *why* they behave that way. On reaching the end of a successful crime novel, readers need not only to have the murderer revealed, but also to understand the motivation that lies behind the murder. What is it in the killer's background that has shaped their personality to make them an assassin?

Then what of the victim? What reason have they given the killer for their death? What is it in their character that has turned them into a corpse? I am not suggesting that they are responsible for their demise but there will be something about them that has attracted death.

Of course, in a crime novel, you do not only have a killer and victim, you have suspects. Your investigator, whether official or unofficial, together with the reader, will discover grounds for wondering about the motivation of several people who have the opportunity and means of committing the crime. Dark secrets and personality defects will be revealed that can provide motivation. The author, though, must never allow the process of the discovery and examination of suspects to appear formulaic. Each character must have a valid place in the story and be made interesting.

Minette Walters' novel, *The Breaker,* opens with the discovery of the body of a naked girl washed up on a beach. The investigation into first who she is, and then who was responsible for her death, is conducted by the police, but the story is told from the point of view of a variety of characters. Soon three suspects emerge and Walters skilfully shifts the emphasis from first one to another and then to the third, and then back again, so that the reader is constantly reassessing their assumptions as they discover more about the characters and the careful uncovering of the events that led up to the death of the victim. It's a dazzling display of psychological suspense and also of police procedure.

Creating interesting and believable characters entails building up a picture of them and their background. For each of my characters I write out what Hollywood calls the 'backstory'. This is an account of their lives before the point where they enter the book; details of their family, what their history is so far, what their character traits are and everything that has formed their personality by the time they appear in the story. The more detailed the biography is, the more I begin to feel I understand and can write about them. Nine-tenths of each of these potted histories never makes it onto the page but it means that each person exists for me. I know how they will react in the situations they are faced with in the story and, hopefully, the reader will find them believable.

Val McDermid talks to her characters, in the car, out shopping, anywhere, so that she can hear their voices in her head.

Martin Edwards begins planning a book, 'by thinking about a motive for murder – a reason to kill a fellow human being that intrigues me and is a little out of the ordinary. So my initial characters, apart from the detective, are a murderer and a victim and it is the characterisation of those individuals that is the starting point for the book. Everything else follows from that.'

Exercise

Take the character you dreamed up for the first exercise in this chapter, look at their personality traits and decide what it is in their past life that has determined or contributed to their current behaviour.

Let's take another look at Paul. His 'back story' could run something like this:

Born into a middle class family in the English Midlands, father a middle-ranking civil servant, disappointed in life, mother a selfish woman who never worked but enjoyed her bridge afternoons. Paul had a brother who was six years older than himself. Vincent was a brilliant scholar and a dynamic sportsman. He was adored by his parents who invested all their hopes for the future in him. As soon as he was old enough, Vincent organised himself adventurous holidays, climbing with friends in the Peak District, rafting in France, a cultural holiday in Florence, etc. Paul finds himself accompanying his parents on their annual bridge holiday in Cornwall. He doesn't particularly want to but cannot seem to find anything better to do. There he spends lonely times on the beach and cycling round the countryside. He reads thrillers, imagining himself as the hero.

Unlike Vincent, who was very attractive, Paul has the sort of appearance that doesn't stand out in any way. Not particularly tall, neither fat nor thin, with mid-brown, thin hair, eyes that are neither grey nor blue, ordinary features, a light, rather hesitant voice.

Vincent gains a scholarship to Oxford and is expected to achieve a First Class Honours degree, but on a skiing holiday in Austria, he is killed by an avalanche. The parents are devastated by the loss of their brilliant son. Everything Paul does is a severe disappointment to them. He can bring no light into their lives. He fails to get into university and becomes an articled clerk, gradually qualifying as a chartered accountant without any recognition of this achievement from his parents. He fails to attract any of the girls whom he finds interesting, and eventually marries a secretary in his office. Quiet, self-effacing and pleasant-looking, Brenda was initially grateful for his interest in her and believes there is much more to him than the rest of the world will allow. After marriage, however, she realises she was mistaken and gradually picks up from his parents a contempt for her husband. She grows to despise what she sees as his negativity and inability to rise to the top. She transmits these feelings to their children. Paul hates the situation but cannot see any way of changing it. He longs to behave how his dead brother did when alive, but cannot bring himself to act in the same way. Less intelligent, he feels himself to be genuinely inferior. He cannot accept that any of his achievements are genuine. This sets up a self-defeating cycle of failure that reinforces his sense of inferiority.

The trigger for Paul's rebellion could be meeting a resourceful and manipulative girl who enables him at last to see himself as the hero of the thriller novels he loves. Between them they develop the idea for making off with large sums of Paul's firm's money. Within Paul there gradually wakens a belief in himself and his ability. When faced with the drowning child, he doesn't hesitate but dives in. What motivates Paul is desperation to shake off his unsatisfactory life. But his life is unsatisfactory because he lacks vision and self-discipline. Eventually this will mean that his attempt to free himself fails.

What about Alice's back-story?

Alice's father is a train driver who takes his responsibilities for passenger safety very seriously. Alice's mother is a care assistant in a local nursing home. Both parents adore Alice and are very proud of how well she does at school and her ability to shine in any activity she takes on. They surround her with love and teach her to be confident. Alice is an only child and her parents want her to have every advantage that they lacked. She grows up assuming that she can do anything she wants and that she deserves the very best of everything.

Alice is awarded a scholarship to Oxford, takes a gap year and travels. Until this point everything in Alice's life has lead her to believe that she is the golden girl who will get whatever she wants and will never have to bear responsibility for her actions. Narrowly escaping jail acts as a wake-up call, not that she is as vulnerable as anyone else – after all, she didn't get caught – but that she needs to be more careful in life.

At Oxford she mixes with students who are as bright as she is, but have a great deal more money. She has an affair with an upper-class boy and gets dumped for someone of his own background. Her pride is more hurt than her heart. The incident fires Alice's determination to succeed. Wealth doesn't attract her, she simply wants power, and to show those who have had a privileged upbringing that she can beat them. Which means she intends being Prime Minister.

Alice's husband is Mark, product of an upwardly mobile working class family. His father has made a minor fortune out of running a haulage company. His mother handles the accountancy side. Mark became a teacher. He meets Alice during her first, unsuccessful, campaign as a parliamentary candidate and loves what he sees as her idealism. She marries him because she loves the way he worships her. What motivates Alice is unbridled ambition.

These are very brief back-stories, there is much more to be noted down about Paul and Alice, but I hope they give you a general idea of how such biographies can be created. The exact form they take doesn't matter, they can be as elaborate or as terse as you like. You can write them as narrative as I have, or under headings such as: family, education, career, personality traits, etc, etc.

Now look at the characters you have created. Have they become believable to you? Can you imagine them doing a serious crime? Does their motivation ring true?

Keith Miles says: 'Know your characters inside out before you commit them to paper. Even relatively minor characters should have depth to them.' He suggests using your main character or characters in a short story before embarking on a full-length novel as 'an ideal way to explore possibilities and to build up confidence'.

Natasha Cooper advises, 'Know your characters before you write the first word. Think (and write) in vivid scenes: where are your characters? What can they see, smell, feel, hear and taste?'

Descriptions

You need to not only understand how your characters behave, but also need to create physical descriptions of them. Writers – and readers – vary in their need to build mental pictures of their characters. Some writers rely on dialogue to create character and give very little actual physical description. Other writers want readers to be able to see their characters with minute precision. With crime writing, painting a picture in words of how a character looks can indicate personality, or hint how a character would like to be viewed.

To each biography, then, you need to add details of what your character looks like: their height, colour of hair and eyes, their body size. If they are fat, are they pleasantly chubby or obese – and how does it affect their personalities? What about their hairstyle? This is particularly important with women, but also counts with men. Balding men can be very sensitive about the disappearance of their hair. Some demonstrate this by the care they take to make the most of whatever they have left. Others defy nature by shaving their heads. And there are those who merely have what is left neatly trimmed. Each of these approaches demonstrates character.

How do your characters dress? Do they try to conform to what they feel will make them feel comfortable in their regular setting? This will demonstrate a desire for acceptance, whether the 'acceptable' rig is twin set and pearls or a punk-rocker outfit. The punk-rocker wants to shock, while the twin-set and pearls' female wants to fit into a more conventional life pattern, but both require the back-up of what is almost a uniform to feel comfortable in their chosen society.

There is the character who wants to walk into any situation and look different from everyone else there. They may buy their clothes at charity shops or second-hand clothes agencies and put together the sort of look they feel demonstrates their personality – or what they want others to think of their personality.

Then there are characters who suddenly change their look. A woman can suddenly throw away the 'mumsy' outfits she has worn for many years, and lash out on high fashion. A man can discard his suits and go in for up-to-the-minute casual gear. Why do these characters behave like this, what does it demonstrate?

Investigators who follow suspects or try to infiltrate closed societies (think private eye, spy stories, gangland situations, etc), always try to dress in a way that won't make them look different either from the background or from their targets. Changing a jacket or scarf, putting on a hat or glasses, can transform the way someone is perceived. Those who try to deceive understand the power of clothes.

Here is how Ian Rankin introduces a new character about half way through *Fleshmarket Close* as one of his series' detectives, Detective Sergeant Siobhan Clarke, meets another detective at the scene of a murder:

> She tried a winning smile. DI Young was just that – young;
> younger than her anyway, and already above her in rank. A sturdy
> face above a sturdier body. Probably played rugby, maybe came

*from farming stock. He had red hair and fairer eyelashes, a few
burst blood vessels either side of his nose. If someone had told her
he wasn't long out of school, she'd probably have believed them.*

Here's a neat little description from *Dying Voices* by Laura
Wilson, an atmospheric story told in the first person. The
narrator visits her gay friend, Tony:

> *Tony's new chauffeur and general factotum, Dominic, was
> sitting at the kitchen table with the guard from the security
> company and his long-haired Alsation, which lay under the table,
> panting and gazing at us with greedy eyes.*
>
> *Dominic turned out to be quite nice in a golden retriever
> sort of way. Tony always goes for men who look like young John
> Kennedys – heavy pink chops and buttery blond hair. Not my cup
> of tea, but there you go.*

Both these descriptions give much more than a list of
physical characteristics. Although they do not spend too
much time on capturing their characters, the reader has a
good idea not only of how they look but also what sort of
people they are.

There are times when characters appear who don't feature
in the plot but are part of a scene and need to be described in
a way that brings both them and the scene to life. As in this
paragraph from Denise Mina's *Garnethill*, where the heroine
is trying to follow the directions she has been given for an
Abusers Anonymous meeting and enters a church:

> *The high altar was a white moulded wall of saints on a background
> of pseudo-Gothic drapery. The front two pews were busy with
> penitents, sitting down awaiting confession or kneeling on the far
> side of the aisle from the confessional boxes with their heads bent
> intently, doing their penance. Just inside the glass wall, on the very
> back bench, knelt a white-haired woman wearing an old-style black
> mantilla. She was saying her rosary, her windswept arthritic fingers
> flicking through the jet beads wrapped around her hand, her lips
> quivering as she received the 'Glory Be', her pious head bent low.*

All of the above descriptions bring the characters to life as
we read them. We can see them as people in a way that a

straightforward itemisation of their features would not have achieved.

I find it helpful to cut out pictures of interesting looking people from newspapers and magazines. These are usually not celebrities but ordinary people, unposed, news shots. I keep them in a special file. Another favourite activity of mine is people-watching. This is an ideal way of passing time when waiting for a bus or a plane, or travelling in a train. Imagining what sort of people passers by and fellow passengers are, and jotting down notes on their appearance, can be very useful.

How his characters look is very important to Michael Jecks and he constantly studies people. 'I make use of people in the streets in cities. Sitting in a café and watching can be incredibly instructive. When I latch onto a face, I make a rough sketch of it on paper, with any obvious characteristics such as shape of the chin, mouth, eyes, cheekbones, and any strange (or what appear to me to be strange) mannerisms. In my books all the potential protagonists have detailed characterisation, which I write up on a giant whiteboard in front of my desk so that they are there, in front of me all the time. Their foibles, characteristic speech patterns, and mannerisms are in the forefront on my mind as I write. It is essential that any action must be credible when set against the main characterisation as displayed on the board.'

Body language

Here is some advice from Alex Gray: 'Why a character acts in a certain way is much more pertinent to a crime novel than to any other type of fiction and so the writer must be fairly conversant with human behaviour. When I first began writing crime fiction I was glad of the advice from experienced veterans of the genre who helped me to see that such things as body language were an essential part of character description. The old adage of "show not tell" takes a step further in crime fiction especially when a trained detective is described observing a potential suspect.'

Make a habit of studying how people show what is going on inside them by the way they use their bodies. Who hasn't seen a friend walking down the street ahead of them and known that they are deeply depressed? Their shoulders sag, their steps lack energy. When you tap them on the shoulder and say hello, though, they can turn and immediately set their shoulders back and greet you with a smile as though everything is right in their world. You know differently. So it is with your characters, and a trained detective will observe body language as carefully as what interviewees say.

Behaviour

Habits – or lack of them – can also highlight character and allow the reader to gather a great deal about a person without it being spelled out to them. Remember the great injunction to fiction writers mentioned by Alex Gray: show, don't tell. For instance, a passage demonstrating how a man spends all his time at the local, while his wife copes with the children at home, says a great deal about both him and their marriage – and does so much more effectively than a statement about what a poor husband he is.

The office girl who is always sneaking off to the ladies to repair her make-up, and comes in late with a carrier bag from a boutique, demonstrates that she minds much more about her appearance than her job.

Exercise

Take a character, perhaps one that you created earlier for this chapter, and write a scene that demonstrates some aspect of them.

Here's my scene: *As I arrived, Mrs Burke was entering the rusty gate that stood open at the end of the path up to her house. I introduced myself and learned that she had been out all day but that her children might have seen something. She slipped her key into the shabby door of her semi-detached house. 'I always tell my kids they must be respectful. There's not enough respect around these days.' The hall was cluttered with abandoned shoes, a couple of satchels and a dropped coat. She picked the coat up, tutting. 'Never take care of their things, I'm always on at them about that.' I followed her through to the kitchen. There two kids of about nine and ten were watching television. A half-eaten loaf stood on the side together with a tub of marge and a nearly empty pot of jam. Two be-crumbed plates and glasses that had contained milk were beside them. I looked at my watch, half-past five. Both kids were in school uniform, neither shirt had been ironed. 'Turn that telly off,' Mrs Burke said sharply. 'You kids got no manners. This is Detective Sergeant Shaw, come to ask if you've seen anything unusual next door this afternoon. You tell her everything that happened since you come home from school, understand?'*

What I wanted to show was that Mrs Burke was a woman who liked to give the impression of respectability but cared little about her house or her children, who were sent off to school in un-ironed shirts and allowed to come home to an empty house.

The breaking of habits can be equally revealing. Take a character who always spends holidays at the same place, perhaps at a non-fashionable seaside resort, then suddenly does something very different – goes on a cruise or flies off to an exotic location. Perhaps they have come into money, or decided it is time to realise a long-held ambition. Whatever it is, the change could be relevant to an investigation into a crime, and the action is an effective way of demonstrating that a sea-change in their lives has taken place.

Equally, the twenty-something who suddenly gives up a life of hedonism, or rebellion, acquires a steady job and looks like settling down, has undergone a Damascene conversion of some kind. What was it? And is the youngster truly reformed or trying to escape unwelcome attention?

Possessions

Where characters live, what their homes look like, what sort of car they drive, if they do, how they spend their spare time, what they spend money on, all these can throw light on the sort of people they are. The entrepreneur who talks big, but drives an aged hatchback, either genuinely does not care about his image or is not nearly as successful as he is trying to make out. Which is it? The well-dressed girl who never has a hair out of place, but lives in a pigsty, is either a slob at heart or is too pressed for time to do her housework. Do dirt and chaos bother her?

Names

Obviously, all characters have to be called something. Choosing names for yours can be as important as choosing names for your children.

Names carry baggage. Often we associate characteristics with the names of people we know. I once knew a girl called Angela. I didn't like her; I thought she was stuck-up, thoughtless and rude. Probably Angela didn't like me. So I can't give that name to any female character I feel sympathetic towards. On the other hand, the names of people I like I would find difficult to give to a murderer or someone very unpleasant.

Names go in and out of fashion. They can demonstrate age, background, class. There are also names that are ageless and classless: John, James, Jane, Sally, for instance.

I can spend a long time deciding on names for my characters. When I wrote my first book, I called my cook-investigator, Penny. Before I finished the book, I discovered that Susan Moody had published several of the sparkling Penny Wanawake series. I decided I had to change my heroine's name. I found it incredibly difficult. My character answered to Penny. I now knew her well but as Penny. She *was* Penny. I had to stop writing the book while I found another name for my cherished chef. I toyed with name after name; none of them seemed to fit my character.

Then I went to Ballymaloe, to the cookery school there and met Darina Allen, who runs it. As I watched this efficient, charming person demonstrating dishes, I turned her name over in my mind. For me, it had no baggage and it belonged to someone who knew and loved food. I went back home and finished my book, changing Penny to Darina. Incidentally, as a novice with a computer, I discovered one of the hazards of using 'find and replace'. Reading through the manuscript some time later, I was surprised to come across: not a Darina more!

There are dictionaries of first names that include provenance and usage and they can be very useful. However, if you have characters with a non-English background, you have to be as careful with naming them as you are with any Anglo-Saxon character.

Surnames can be as difficult as first names. They, too, carry baggage. Also, there is the danger of giving someone a full name that belongs to someone in real life. By itself it mightn't cause problems but if, by some awful mischance, you gave the name to a murderer with a description much the same as the real person, you might be laying yourself open to unpleasant consequences. There are professional lists for some professions that can be checked out, which can ensure you haven't given a real-life name to your unpleasant doctor, lawyer, MP or local councillor. You should always check the electoral roll in the area in which you set your story and/or where the character lives and if you find there is someone with the same name as your character, change the name of your character. Readers not present in the UK may be surprised to hear that England and Wales have some of the most severe libel laws in the world and authors do get sued.

Take care with naming historical characters. They should fit easily into the period of your book, yet not be too difficult for the reader to get hold of.

Some writers try to avoid giving a character a real name by going to a map book for surnames. It's a practice that goes back a long way. Towards the end of the nineteenth century, the San Francisco-born writer John Griffith Chaney called himself Jack London. Peter Walker gives a tip for finding apt names for characters. He trawls the births and deaths columns of local newspapers and simply amalgamates one or two to create a name. Keith Miles recommends avoiding long names for major characters: 'You may have to type them out hundreds of times in the course of a novel. It will tire you and irritate the reader.'

Whatever method you choose, watch that you do not have a set of names that either all start with the same first letter, or sound the same. It is astonishing how easy it is to find you have called your characters Martin, Mark, Matthew, Mary, Melinda and Maggie. Unless there is some plot reason why initials should be duplicated, try and ensure names do not follow a pattern. Apart from anything else, it can be very confusing for readers.

Make a list of dramatis personae as you write your book, it can be very helpful. It will save having to look back through your work to check what you called that minor character who is now popping up again. And it will avoid duplication of names and initials.

When you introduce a character in your book, make sure that, unless there is some very good plot reason why not, you introduce them by name. The reader wants to be able to identify them and know without doubt when they reappear.

An important part of knowing your characters is being able to capture their speech. And dialogue is the subject of the next chapter.

Characterisation & motivation

> ➤ Understand what lies beneath the surface appearance of your characters
> ➤ Work out back stories for your characters, why they have become the people they are by the time they appear in your book
> ➤ Write full physical descriptions of your characters
> ➤ Think about how a person's appearance can reflect their personality – or what they hope will be thought of their personality
> ➤ Changes in appearance or habits can demonstrate a plot point in your characters
> ➤ Show characteristics in action/dialogue rather then telling the reader about them

> ➤ Collect pictures and descriptions of interesting characters
> ➤ Note body language and use it
> ➤ Take care when naming characters
> ➤ Make a list of your characters as they appear

Dialogue

Dialogue is a vital part of creating character and an essential part of a successful book. This is particularly true for a crime novel, which has to find effective ways of conveying investigative details to the reader. How good is your ear for the way people speak?

Exercise

Here is a very simple exercise. Write a sentence or two for each of the following characters telling a friend that they don't want to go to a party:

a) An elderly woman
b) A teenage boy
c) A thirty-year old salesman
d) A forty-year old woman-about-town

How hard did you think about the person you were writing the dialogue for? Were you able to dash off the sentences quickly or did it take you some time to bring to mind how each person would talk? Look at what you have written. If nothing else told you, would you know what sort of person was speaking?

Here is my effort:

a) 'You go without me, dear, somehow I don't feel up to a party tonight.'
b) 'No way! Man, you is dissin me ain't yer.'
c) 'Wouldn't be seen dead there, chum. Anyway, met a corker today I reckon will be up for it.'
d) 'Honestly, darling, those people are so last year and when that bitch, Jackie, saw my new Armani suit she said M & S was really coming up trumps these days.'

These can be seen as stereotypical and are unlikely to be effective in a well-written novel, but I hope they indicate how character can be reflected in a simple sentence.

As well as illustrating character, dialogue can also be used to inform the reader.

Developments in an investigation can be discussed between colleagues. Think of Holmes talking cases over with Dr Watson; Poirot with Captain Hastings. Watson and Hastings could be described as stooges. Today, an investigator tends to have a partner who is more of an equal. Detectives need not be of the same rank but each will contribute ideas and information. The exchanges between Ian Rankin's *Rebus* and several of his colleagues, most especially with Siobhan Clarke, provide fine examples. But information can be given through conversations between all sorts of different characters and dialogue is one of the most important tools in a crime writer's equipment.

Take the following exchange between a brother and sister, both directors of a publishing house, very early on in P D James's *Original Sin*. All that has happened so far is the discovery of the body of a colleague who has committed suicide.

> *'Claudia, it's pointless to reopen all those old arguments. It was necessary to sack her and I sacked her. That had nothing to do with her death. I did what had to be done in the interests of the firm and at the time you agreed. Neither you nor I can be blamed for her suicide and her death has nothing to do with the other mischief here either.' He paused then said: 'Unless of course she was the one responsible.'*
>
> *She didn't miss the sudden note of hope in his voice. So he was more worried than he would admit. She said bitterly: 'That would be a neat way out of our troubles, wouldn't it? But how could she have been, Gerard? She was off sick, remember, when the Stilgo proofs were tampered with and visiting an author in Brighton when we lost the illustrations for the Guy Fawkes book. No, she's in the clear.'*

There is a wealth of information given in this short exchange and the alert reader will pick it all up.

In a completely different style but, again, filling in the reader on information, is this excerpt from Ian Rankin's *The Hanging Garden*.

Detective Inspector Rebus, Rankin's loner series character, and two colleagues have been on surveillance duty at a well-known criminal hang-out when an injured man is deposited from a speeding car onto the road. In helping him, Rebus's shirt is covered in blood and at the hospital where the injured man is taken, a doctor lends him a garish T shirt. He gives Detective Sergeant Claverhouse a drink from a quarter bottle of whisky he carries; he doesn't take one himself, he's on the wagon. Then they leave the cloakroom to rejoin Detective Constable Siobhan Clarke:

> They walked back to A&E. Siobhan Clarke was waiting for them outside a closed door.
>
> 'They've had to sedate him' she said. 'He was up on his feet again, reeling all over the place.' She pointed to marks on the floor – airbrushed blood, smudged by footprints.
>
> 'Do we have a name?'
>
> 'He's not offered one. Nothing in his pockets to identify him. Over two hundred in cash, so we can rule out a mugging. What do you reckon for a weapon? Hammer?'
>
> Rebus shrugged. 'A hammer would dent the skull. That flap looked too neat. I think they went for him with a cleaver.'
>
> 'Or a machete,' Claverhouse added. 'Something like that.'
>
> Clarke stared at him. 'I smell whisky.'
>
> Claverhouse put a finger to his lips.
>
> 'Anything else?' Rebus asked. It was Clarke's turn to shrug.
>
> 'Just one observation.'
>
> 'What's that?'
>
> 'I like the t-shirt.'

That exchange informs the reader of the facts known and supposed about the injured man. It also says a good deal about the three detectives. There is an inspector, a sergeant and a constable but they are comfortable with each other, share camaraderie and are able to discuss a case on equal terms.

If you find writing dialogue easy and love dreaming up snappy retorts and passages that scintillate with clever remarks, you are blessed. Beware, though, of letting the smart chitchat rattle along without it actually doing anything more than simply amuse the reader. Too much of that and the reader will lose interest.

Remember that dialogue should have a purpose. It should do at least one of the following and often more than one:

> ➢ Reveal character
> ➢ Develop the plot
> ➢ Make information interesting
> ➢ Increase or relax tension
> ➢ Assist in the creation of atmosphere

Exercise

Write a scene between two characters talking together. Their conversation should reveal something about themselves and also move a crime plot forward.

Did you have your couple arguing? Disagreements between people can increase tension. Also, when arguing, people tend to get emotional, lose some of their control and can let slip something they would prefer to have kept to themselves. People who have just had an unfortunate experience, perhaps finding a murder victim, will also reveal more of themselves than they would normally.

Maybe, instead, you had your couple discussing how the murder investigation was going. Maybe one of them has one theory and the other a different one. Or perhaps one is telling the other of some new development. Do they have clearly defined characters that come through in their dialogue?

Perhaps one of your characters has discovered something about the other one and is trying to establish whether it is true or not. There could be prevarication or anger on the part of the suspect, or an attempt to foil the questioner or feed them false information.

Or you may have written something completely different from any of the above. It doesn't matter what, as long as it moves the plot forward and reveals something of the two characters.

Eavesdropping

If you have trouble with dialogue, listen to people talking, in shops, in cafés and restaurants, in public transport, in the street. Sometimes you can pick up a chance phrase that seems to sum up a character or situation, or that seems too good to forget. That is the time to get out your notebook and jot it down. It is unusual to know exactly how such phrases can be used as you make notes, but you can be sure that the time will come when it will prove the perfect piece of dialogue.

A piece of advice from Keith Miles: 'Remember that every person has an individual speech rhythm so dialogue must never be interchangeable between characters.'

Peter Lovesey discovered when writing *On the Edge,* a black comedy set in 1946 about two women who murder their husbands (later televised as *Dead Gorgeous*), that he had little idea about how women talk to each other when their husbands aren't around. He needed a lot of help with that particular dialogue from his wife, Jax. He says his approach was much too decorous and timid.

Good dialogue on the page doesn't always copy exactly how people speak in real life. Eavesdropping can reveal that people usually talk in unfinished phrases, indulge in constant repetition, assume that the person they are talking to understands exactly what they are referring to when to the eavesdropper it is far from clear. A book that faithfully replicated how people actually speak would be extremely difficult to read. But dialogue should be realistic. Here is an excerpt from John Harvey's *Flesh and Blood,* a book in which he introduces Detective Inspector Frank Elder, who has taken early retirement. Elder gets caught up in new developments in an old case, developments which draw in his family, ex-wife Joanne and daughter Katherine. John Harvey is a very subtle writer; his characterisation is always believable and looks beyond the obvious. This short passage is a flashback explanation of how Elder's marriage broke up, years after he'd thought it had survived a difficult patch:

> *Eight years down the line, Katherine on the point of starting secondary school, Joanne was offered the chance to manage a new salon Miles was opening in Nottingham. They moved again. Settled in. Katherine was happy in her new school. Elder had slipped into the Major Crime Unit with relative ease. Sometimes you never saw it coming until it was too late.*
>
> *'I've been seeing him again. Martyn. I'm sorry, Frank, I . . .'*
>
> *'Seeing him?'*
>
> *'Yes. Frank, I'm sorry, I. . .'*
>
> *'How long?'*
>
> *'Frank. . .'*
>
> *'How long have you been seeing him?'*
>
> *'Frank, please. . .'*
>
> *Elder's whisky spilled across the back of his hand, the tops of his thigh. 'How fucking long?'*
>
> *'Oh, Frank. . .Frank. . .' Joanne in tears now, her breath uneven, her face wiped clear of colour. 'We never really stopped.'*

Despite the shortness of the exchange, the brevity of each side of the conversation, and without knowing much of the background, the reader can recognise each of the participants, the information given without any elaboration or underlining, and the truth of the short phrases. John Harvey is not a writer who wastes words and the insights gained into both Frank Elder and his ex-wife will be built on later in the plot.

Using dialogue to develop plot

Look back at the chapter on plotting. An effective crime novel does not follow a straight path. It twists and turns, so that the reader is led to focus first on one aspect of the plot, and then on another, as fresh developments are introduced. When new characters appear, dialogue can be an effective way both of transmitting information and revealing character.

Exercise

A new character appears in your story. Your investigator hasn't met this person before. Write a few lines of dialogue that will reveal something of the new personality and also show that the investigator finds them suspicious.

Get hold of a copy of Robert Wilson's *A Small Death in Lisbon* (publisher HarperCollins, 1999, ISBN 0 00 651202 X), and read the interview between a respected lawyer, the father of a teenage girl who has been murdered, and the detective and his assistant who are in charge of the case. It is too long to quote here but the passage is a fine example of a conversation that both reveals, through facts concerning the murdered girl and the lawyer's relationship with her, and conceals through lack of reaction on the part of the policemen to what they are being told. The scene is written through the eyes of the detective, who only listens, trying to hide his surprise at the lawyer's dispassionate recital of what are shocking details. Readers are left to draw their own conclusions regarding what they are being told; they are not nudged to take notice at any point. It takes most of the book for the full import of this long, detailed interview to become clear and demonstrate how cleverly the lawyer tempered what he told the detectives. It is a fine example of subtle story-telling.

Make information interesting

Detail that the reader needs to be informed about can be made more interesting by being included in dialogue. For instance, here is a passage from Reginald Hill's novel, *Good Morning, Midnight*. A man has committed suicide by blowing his head off with a shotgun behind a locked door, precisely as his father had committed suicide ten years earlier. Detective Superintendent, Andrew Dalziel, is filling in Detective Chief Inspector Peter Pascoe with a complicated piece of background, which is essential to the story. Having dealt with the development of a machine tool firm in the Second World War and after by Liam, the suicide's grandfather, and called the suicide Pal Junior and his father, Pal Senior, Andrew Dalziel continues:

> '*Pal Senior had an education, nowt special, but enough to set him up as an English gent. Did all the things gents are supposed*

to do, like tearing foxes into shreds and blowing small birds to smithereens.'

'Which is how he had the shotgun to blow himself to pieces?'

'Aye. Could've been one of the birds fought back, of course. No, we'd have noticed the bird shit. Gave all that up in his thirties when he had his accident.'

'Shooting accident?'

'No. As well as huntin' and shootin', he were a bit of a climber in every sense. Yon painting in there shows him at his peak, that's a joke. You know how those mad buggers like to make life difficult for themselves. Well, he were the first to climb some Scottish cliff, solo, at midnight, on Christmas Day, bollock naked, or summat like that.'

There is much more and all of it amusing and telling. Reginald Hill has used Andy Dalziel's basic humour and deliberately non-intellectual, man-of-the-people approach to inform the reader both about background and also to give a flavour of Dalziel himself. With a series there will always be new readers who have to be introduced to characters other readers know well.

Relax or tighten tension

There is a limit to the amount of tension a reader can take. Dialogue can introduce a lighter note, allowing a moment's breathing space, before the writer tightens it again.

In Denise Mina's *Garnethill*, Maureen discovers the extremely bloody body of her lover in her living room, at the very time she had decided that the affair was over. After being interrogated by the police, she goes to a friend, Benny, for refuge.

She sat back down at the table. 'It turns out they were married, after all. I feel like such a mug.'

'Douglas was married to Elsbeth?'

'Yeah.'

He touched her forearm and spoke softly. 'I thought ye'd decided he was an arse anyway.'

'Yeah,' she said miserably, 'but he was my arse.'

That last line lifts the atmosphere.

Snappy dialogue can be used to build tension. Short sentences, sometimes forced out from a character's mouth, can speed the reader's eye and help to create pace.

Accents

The moment you hear a Scotsman, or an Irishman, or the owner of a regional accent speak, you know immediately where they are from. The same goes for foreign accents. Putting them over in a book, though, can cause problems.

Some authors go to immense trouble to use phonetic spelling to reproduce an accent on the page. This can make the text very difficult to read and prove off-putting. However, a touch every now and then can place a speaker. 'It's no' a . . .' or 'awa wi' ye', for instance, will instantly place the speaker as Scottish.

The best way to capture an accent is to recognise the rhythm of local speech. The order of words can be as revealing as their sound. For instance, the Irish have a habit of ending sentences with a question. 'And isn't that the truth of it?' In Somerset a local is likely to say, 'Wait you off there', and personalise inanimate objects; a broken down tractor can be referred to as, ''E won't run.' Look again at the excerpt above from *Good Morning, Midnight*. Dalziel's Yorkshire accent comes through clearly and it's shown through choice of words and the rhythm of his speech rather than phonetic spelling.

Historical dialogue

Crime novels set in a previous period are popular; readers seem to love getting beneath the skin of a different age and historical crime novels have an ability to transport the reader to another period and make it come alive that can be very attractive.

That very immediacy poses a problem when it comes to dialogue. In an effort to make characters relevant for modern readers, some authors forgo period flavour for idiomatic ways of speaking that reflect contemporary speech patterns.

Each author has to make their own choice but, when enormous effort has been made to create a picture of a previous time, it can be disconcerting to find characters talking as though they live in the present day. However, what one could call a 'gadzooks' approach, lacing the dialogue with stereotypical period phrases such as 'Pray, sir, do tell', does not do much to conjure a past era for the reader.

I have written a series of three historical crime novels set in the mid-eighteenth century and my approach has been somewhere between the two.

In researching the first of these books, I read the novels of Henry Fielding, whose brother was the 'blind judge', Sir John Fielding, the Bow Street magistrate who was responsible for creating the Bow Street runners in the middle of the eighteenth century.

Letters were another source. Written language is never the same as spoken but some letters can be very colloquial and certainly reflect the vocabulary of the times. Andrew Taylor says one should be wary of confusing the formal approach with the informal when consulting contemporary sources. Not all letters are colloquial.

I also found some records of ecclesiastical court cases that contained what seemed to be verbatim reports of witnesses that yielded a considerable vocabulary of swear words.

All these sources would, I hoped, accustom my ear to the idiomatic speech of my period and produce dialogue which didn't sound artificial but was firmly grounded in the eighteenth century.

C J Sansom's novel, *Dark Fire,* which won the 2005 Ellis Peters Historical Crime Dagger, is set in 1540. In it, Lawyer Matthew Shardlake (note the name, it belongs perfectly to the period) is applied to by a previous client of his for help. Joseph Wentworth's young niece has been accused of murdering her cousin. The lawyer, doubtful if he can help, goes to visit Wentworth, a farmer in Essex:

> *His face brightened as he saw me, and he came over and shook my hand eagerly. 'Master Shardlake! Good day, good day. You had my letter?'*

'I did. You are staying in London?'

'At an inn down by Queenhithe,' he said. 'My brother has forbidden me his house for my championing of our niece.' There was a desperate look in his hazel eyes. 'You must help me, sir, please. You must help Elizabeth.'

I decided no good would be done by beating round the bushes. I took the pamphlet from my pocket and handed it to him.

'Have you seen this, Joseph?'

'Yes.' He ran a hand through his curly black hair. 'Are they allowed to say these things? Is she not innocent until proven guilty?'

He took a delicately embroidered handkerchief from his pocket and mopped his brow. 'I visited Elizabeth in Newgate this morning,' he said. 'God's mercy, it's a terrible place. But she still won't talk.' He ran a hand over his plump, badly shaven cheeks. 'Why won't she talk? It's her only hope of saving herself.' He looked across at me pleadingly, as though I had the answer. I raised a hand.

'Come, Joseph, sit down. Let us start at the beginning. I know only what you told me in your letter, which is little more than is in this foul pamphlet.'

The only period phrase that sticks out is 'God's mercy' but the rhythm of the speech conveys a feeling of the times. It is more formal than we use today but still has a colloquial quality.

Here is an excerpt from another Ellis Peters Historical Dagger winner, Andrew Taylor's *The American Boy*. Set in 1819/1820, the book is a densely-layered, complex mystery with Dickensian qualities. It opens with the narrator, Thomas Shield, arriving for an interview with the Reverend Mr Bransby for a badly-needed job as a tutor in a boys' school. The only reference he has is from his aunt and Mr Bransby is not impressed:

'It is true that your aunt, Mrs Reynolds, was the best housekeeper my parents ever had. As a boy I never had any reason to doubt her veracity or indeed her kindness. But those two facts do not necessarily encourage me to allow a lunatic and a drunkard a position of authority over the boys entrusted to my care.'

'Sir, I am neither of those things.'

He glared at me. 'A man, moreover, whose former employers will not speak for him.'

> *'But my aunt speaks for me. If you know her, sir, you will know*
> *she would not do that lightly.'*

Both vocabulary and rhythms, not only of this exchange but also the narrative of the book, catch the tone of the times in which the story is set, yet contain nothing stereotypical. And the characters of both men are contained in their dialogue. *Mr Bransby* does, in fact, employ *Thomas Sheild*. After the interview he summons the American boy of the title, the young Edgar Allan Poe, a student, to meet him [at the academy. Throughout the increasingly tangled, mysterious and compelling events that *Sheild* narrates, the author maintains the beautifully judged period tone that never obtrudes upon the reader yet convinces that the work has indeed been written nearly two hundred years ago.

Finally, I can't resist including a snippet from a novel shortlisted for the Ellis Peters award, *After the Armistice Ball* by Catriona McPherson. This entertaining book is set amongst Scottish high society after the First World War. *Dandy Gilver,* bored with life and with her husband, *Hugh,* is rung up by old friend *Daisy* with a request to help get to the bottom of the disappearance of some famous diamonds:

> *'Sort it,' said Daisy. 'As that divine nanny of yours used to say.*
> *Sort it. Get to the bottom of it, then take a deep breath and tell us*
> *all. Preferably at dinner. Throw your head back and howl. I give*
> *you carte blanche, because of course it's all nonsense and we can't*
> *actually be in a compromising position. Ask Hugh to tell you about*
> *it, then come on Friday and sort it for me.'*

Again, all the flavour of society in the twenties is there.

Read dialogue out loud

The best test of dialogue is to read it out loud. It is the easiest way to identify over-elaborate sentences, clumsy phrases, and anything that somehow jars. It is surprising how prose the eye can skim over quite happily in a silent reading can be revealed as clunky, or even as impossible to speak, when it is read out loud. This method can help enormously for testing the text in the whole of your book – but for dialogue it is essential.

Exercise

Write a short contemporary scene with a police officer interrogating a suspect on their whereabouts at the time of a murder.

Now rewrite the same scene but set it in the second half of the nineteenth century.

Look at the two scenes. Have you shown not only a difference in the way each character speaks but also a difference in the attitude of both policeman and suspect?

Keith Miles suggests that if you do not have a facility for dialogue you set yourself exercises that will help you develop it (more of what I have suggested in this chapter). Then he offers a tip: 'Transpose the opening chapter of your novel, or a short story, into a radio play so that everything has to be told in dialogue form. Or simply write a radio play that is complete in itself. Above all, listen to people and note their conversational mannerisms.'

Having looked at dialogue, the next area that needs to be explored before starting to write your crime novel is background. This is the subject of the next chapter.

Dialogue

> Dialogue must do one of the following:
>> a) Reveal character
>> b) Develop the plot
>> c) Make information interesting
>> d) Increase or relax tension
>> e) Help create atmosphere
> Practice eavesdropping
> Appreciate how rhythm of speech can reflect character and also regional accents
> Try to convey period dialogue without using stereotypical phrases
> Read dialogue out loud

6 Backgrounds and Specialist Knowledge

This chapter is going to look at the world in which you set your crime story and the specialist knowledge that can be used.

Every story has to be set in a particular world. Colin Dexter's *Inspector Morse* novels took place in Oxford but it was *Morse's* particular world, his failure with women, his love of opera, and his idiosyncratic approach to police work, which set their atmosphere and made them unique. Denise Mina's *Garnethill* uses the world of those who wrestle with their mental stability. P D James in *Devices and Desires* explores the world of nuclear protest as well as that of a serial killer.

So location is not the only sort of background that can provide fertile atmosphere and incident to a crime story. Professional or social backgrounds can be equally inspirational.

The background against which your story will unfold will help create atmosphere, can aid your characters' motivation, provide interesting places in which to set scenes, and even inspire ideas for action.

Specialist backgrounds & series characters

If you intend writing a series of crime novels featuring the same character, they have to be able to encounter crime regularly. No problem if they are a detective or a private eye. If not, they should be pursuing the sort of life that will bring them into contact with a wide series of characters – and corpses. Someone who mixes in a small circle of colleagues and friends, who goes to the same work-place every day and leads a circumscribed life, might encounter one crime, but the author is going to find it difficult to involve them in a second and, even more so, in a third.

That is one of the reasons why I chose a cook as the reluctant investigator in my series of culinary crimes. Cooks can move from job to job. One moment they can be providing the food for an historical banquet, in another be working in a restaurant, judging a cookery competition or appearing on television. The different areas of the cookery world offer endless possibilities for encountering chicanery and crime. Each book in the series provides another kind of cookery background from which the story arises.

Jonathan Gash very successfully uses the world of antiques with his *Lovejoy* novels. Michael Ridpath explores the financial world, and demonstrates what a wealth of crime and corruption can surround the making and moving of money.

Another writer who uses the art world, John Malcolm, warns: 'The fascination induced by a specialist background can run away with the plot. Remember that you are writing a drama. The art, orchids, cookery, horse racing, antiques, photography, technology, gambling, period history, politics, whatever, are only the background to that drama.'

Simon Brett has written a series of crime novels involving a none-too-successful actor, Charles Parris, and the theatrical world. Quinton Jardine is the author of an effervescent series with a rather more successful actor, Oz Blackstone.

Remember that the more interesting the background, the easier it is to involve the reader in wanting to find out more. A council worker collecting rubbish may get around, but it would be difficult to involve the reader in that world beyond, perhaps, one gritty novel.

Does the amateur sleuth have a place in the modern crime novel?

Judith Cutler says: 'Much as I love writing about amateur sleuths, I find it increasingly hard to produce a whole series of their adventures. Statistically most of us don't get to investigate any sort of crime in the course of our lives, so while I'm prepared to believe that an observant painter and decorator or keen-eye restaurateur might well get involved in solving one crime – and I loved writing about them doing it! – I know that in reality they wouldn't do it repeatedly. If they did, for goodness' sake, the local constabulary would be investigating them.'

Jessica Mann, though, thinks that the amateur detective definitely still has a place in modern crime fiction; otherwise, she says, the police procedural could become the only remaining form. She adds that, 'There is no place for an amateur working with the police as Sherlock Holmes or Lord Peter Wimsey did, a scenario that was actually quite implausible in their day too.'

Martin Edwards believes that, 'Amateur detectives are not, perhaps, as popular as they were. An obvious problem is that of creating a series where a non-professional can credibly come across mysterious murder time and time again. But, frankly, is it much more likely that a professional such as Inspector Morse would come across so many ingenious crimes in the course of his career?' The same could probably be said of Ian Rankin's Inspector Rebus, but for the reader, murder is much more likely to come a police officer's way than that of a person who lacks any official connection with crime.

Here's Ann Granger: 'I've used both (amateur and official). The advantage of the amateur is a degree of freedom of action, not being bound by the rules. The disadvantage is that modern amateurs can't go round blatantly interfering in police enquiries like Poirot or Lord Peter Wimsey. Also they don't have access to gathered evidence, forensic reports or police records. Where they can come up trumps is in talking to people. Many people will talk more freely to an ordinary person than to a uniform or plainclothes officer. There are categories of people who won't talk to the police on principle or because they don't want to be drawn into the limelight. One of my series detectives, Fran Varady, has as her greatest strength that she is seen as non-threatening and unofficial. At street level where she largely operates people are certainly more likely to co-operate with her. But in the end, in most cases, she has to hand her finds over to the police.'

Zoe Sharp says, 'However good or bad the plot is, if the characters don't come across as real people – ones you care about and would like to know better – you might read the first book in the series, but would probably not come back for more.'

Zoe went for what could be seen as an unusual background for her series character: 'Right from when my grandmother gave me an old 1930's edition of one of Leslie Charteris's The Saint books, I've loved reading crime. It always vaguely irritated me, though, that the heroines seemed to wait around – screaming and spraining their ankles at inopportune moments – until they were rescued by the hero. I wanted something different. And so, eventually, I decided to write it myself.

'Hence Charlotte "Charlie" Fox was born – an ex-Special Forces trainee turned self-defence instructor, who goes on to become a bodyguard. I wrote for purely selfish reasons – this was the kind of character I wanted to read about. And the spur that made me actually start writing my first crime novel? Death threats in the course of my work as a magazine photo-journalist. Nothing like having someone telling you they know where you are and your days are numbered to kick-start the imagination, I found!'

Zoe's actual background, that of a magazine photo-journalist could be ideal for an amateur investigator. Lesley Grant-Adamson has written a series round a journalist. Russell James advises, 'Today's equivalent to the amateur detective is someone who, while not a detective personally, is in a job associated with crime – working perhaps as a journalist, a pathologist, a profiler or even, as with one of Rebecca Tope's fictional heroes, as an undertaker. With such a character the author has a credible hero outside the law itself – and thus presented with more obstacles than someone authorised to investigate – but close enough to be pulled into a long line of future stories.'

Russell might also have mentioned a lawyer. Michael Gilbert wrote his acclaimed mysteries round a solicitor and Martin Edwards also uses a legal background.

The easiest background to employ is one that you have some personal knowledge of. If you have worked as an auctioneer, for instance, or in the theatre, on a cruise ship, or in any area that involves contact with a large number of changing characters, then think seriously about setting a series of novels there. If you haven't any such experience, or, like Zoe, have a yen for some completely different background, don't despair. It is possible to research a potentially rewarding specialist world for your ongoing protagonist.

Remember also Hilary Hale's suggestion that a series can be linked by place or profession rather than a single character.

Your research has to be thorough, it is the small details that build up a persuasive picture and capture the reader's imagination. Reading books, especially autobiographies of people who are or have been involved in your chosen area, can be very helpful. But remember that these backgrounds can change quickly and, unless you are writing a novel set in the past, you will need current information.

As well as reading, remember that there is no substitute for talking to someone who really knows the inside story. They will tell you things you could never find in books or articles; especially details that are valuable to the crime writer: the dodges people get up to, tensions that can arise in the work place, incidents that can throw an unfamiliar light on how a particular world operates.

I once had an illuminating conversation with a specialist food importer that gave me lots of ideas for a book set in that world.

If you can get yourself invited on a tour that will show you exactly what goes on in your chosen area or, even better, find a job you can do there for a short period of time, that, too, will give you unique insights.

When I was wanting to set one of my Darina Lisle books in the television world, I wrote to Peter Bazalgette, then producing the weekly BBC programme, *Food and Drink,* and asked if I could attend the recording of one of the programmes for background colour and information. He said in reply that if I could promise there wouldn't be a dead body on the studio floor afterwards, I was welcome. It was an illuminating day spent watching quietly in the wings, so to speak, and noting everything that went on. I was also at various stages able to speak to most of the people involved in the filming.

How do you find people to interview or to ask if you may have a look at what they do?

It's not as difficult as you might imagine. Most people love talking about their work, and for them to find someone genuinely interested in every aspect of their world can be very attractive. And they are usually thrilled with the idea that they can help with the writing of a book.

Asking everybody you know if they have a contact in the particular area you want to research very often yields someone willing to talk to you.

If you can't get an introduction through a contact, don't be afraid of approaching a professional direct. As I said, most people love talking about what they do. A short letter explaining what you are writing and how they can help together with a request for an interview will very often yield results.

Do some research beforehand so that you know the right questions to get them talking. If you are approaching a company for information, try to get a specific name to write to rather than simply a job title.

John Malcolm has another piece of advice: 'Don't get carried away by your research. You can easily bore the reader with chunks of, to you, fascinating information. Theoretically you should only do the research necessary for the plot. The trouble is that the specialist research itself often suggests further machinations. It needs control.'

Looking for tension and discord

When you are researching a background, be aware of possibilities for discord in your chosen world, ways in which your characters can take advantage of others or come into conflict with them. Perhaps they can frustrate someone's ambitions, find ways to cheat, pursue illegal means, do others down, sabotage, aid rivals, anything that can be useful for your ends.

Your contact may not be aware of such possibilities; you have to be imaginative or look at what you are being shown with a special eye. People can sometimes be taken aback at what you can discern. I called the book set in the television world *Death at the Table,* and sent a copy of it to Peter Bazalgette. He thanked me and said that he had never realised how much scope for tension the programme offered! This does not mean that it was actually there at the time.

For instance, the star cook of the show, Michael Barry, (aka Michael Bukht OBE, he was also formerly a broadcasting executive) had an assistant who prepared all the ingredients for the dishes he demonstrated. As far as I could see that day, they had a very good working relationship. But what if, I wondered, the star chef didn't appreciate all of his assistant's hard work? A conflict situation could easily build up over a series of programmes.

Once someone has been helpful, always give them an acknowledgement in a foreword to your book and send them a copy of the published work.

Specialised knowledge

Apart from finding out about the details of your specialised background, there are other areas you will need to research, such as:

Murder methods & forensic science

Most crime stories hinge on the despatch of victims. How are you going to kill yours and how much do you know about ways of dealing with death? And how much do you know about what forensics will discover after the police have been called in?

Exercise

Imagine a way of killing a victim and write a description of the actual method. Make it as detailed as possible. Then work out how much forensics can reveal both about the murder and the murderer.

Descriptions of death

Death inflicted by an outside agent is a crime and the writer must not flinch from any aspect of the business of discovering a corpse, or of the effects on all concerned. Those unfortunate enough to come upon the body; those who have to deal with it in an official capacity; the friends and relations of the corpse, all to a greater or lesser degree will suffer and the writer has to enter into their feelings.

If the body is discovered by someone unconnected with the victim, a passer-by perhaps, the effect will be very different from that on a loved one or close acquaintance. The officials concerned with the examination of the scene and the investigation will have developed methods for distancing themselves from the scene. The writer needs to examine carefully how each will react and convey their feelings to the reader. Sometimes those feelings will not be what is expected.

When it comes to describing the corpse, the writer has a choice. Every lurid detail can be etched on the reader's consciousness, or the horror can be conveyed without dwelling on gory details.

Compare these two accounts of the discovery of a corpse:

Douglas was tied into the blue kitchen chair with several strands of rope. His throat had been cut clean across, right back to the vertebrae, his head was sitting off centre from his neck. Splashes and spurts of his blood were drying all over the carpet. One long red splatter extended four feet diagonally from the chair, slashing across the arm of the settee and nearly hitting the skirting board on the far wall.

She couldn't seem to move. She was very hot. She had been scuttling back down the hall from the toilet when the blood-drenched cagoule lying just inside the living-room door caught her eye. A trail of bloody footprints led to Douglas, tied to the chair in the dead centre of the room. The footprints were small and regular, like a dance-step diagram.

*She didn't remember sliding down the wall into a foetal crouch.
She must have been there for a while because her backside was
numb. She couldn't see him now, just the cagoule and two of the
footprints but the sweet heavy smell of blood hung like a fog in the
warm hall. The yellow plastic cagoule was drenched in blood. The
hood had been kept up; the blood pattern on the rim was jagged
and irregular.*

*He could have been there all night, she thought. She'd gone
straight to bed when she got in. She'd slept in the same house as
this.*

*Eventually, she got up and phoned the police. 'There's a dead
man in my living-room. It's my boyfriend.'*

Garnethill by Denise Mina

No need to say that this description is full of blood. It also
conveys graphically but economically the effect of this
discovery on Maureen, the protagonist of the book.

Here is Rebus arriving at a crime scene set on a high rise
estate on the edge of Edinburgh:

*There were a dozen figures shuffling around in the covered
walkway between two of the high-rise blocks. The place smelled
faintly of urine, human or otherwise. Plenty of dogs in the vicinity,
one or two even wearing collars. They would come sniffing at the
entrance to the walkway, until chased off by one of the uniforms.
Crime-scene tape now blocked both ends of the passage. Kids on
bikes were craning their necks for a look. Police photographers were
gathering evidence, vying for space with the forensic team. They
were dressed in white overalls, heads covered. An anonymous grey
van was parked alongside the police cars on the muddy play area
outside . . . already they knew they were dealing with homicide.
Multiple stab wounds, including one to the throat. The trail of
blood showed that the victim had been attacked ten or twelve feet
further into the passage. He'd probably tried to get away, crawling
towards the light, his attacker making more lunges as he faltered
and fell.*

Fleshmarket Close by Ian Rankin

Not nearly so much blood and Rebus is an observer unconnected with the corpse, but the tragedy of the scene is well conveyed.

The great crime writer Julian Symons said that the easiest way for an author to commit murder in a book was to push the victim off a cliff. Even then, however, the police will have to establish time of death; examine the scene on the cliff to try to find out if the victim was alone at the time of their fall or if there'd been someone else there; then the corpse will have to undergo a post mortem examination to establish whether death was caused solely by the fall or whether other factors were involved, such as a blow to the head, or the ingestion of poison. Identity has to be established, clothes examined in case they contain clues that may suggest death resulted not from suicide or accident but something more sinister.

However simple a method that is chosen to despatch a victim, there will be medical traces and it is almost inevitable in a crime novel that details of forensic science will feature. In the case of a suspicious death, the police are always going to be called in. Once a crime is reported, the scene is gone over by a SOCO (Scenes of Crime Officers) team. I'm sure you will have seen on television the white-overalled officers conducting their searches. You, as author, can choose how much detail you want to include in your book.

If it's a police procedural, some authors revel in all the background detail on the technical side of an investigation. If you choose to have an unofficial main protagonist, what might be called an 'amateur detective', or a private investigator, a PI, much of this can be avoided.

The science of forensics in the modern world can call upon a vast number of sophisticated techniques. Various television programmes such as the American *CSI* or the British *Waking the Dead,* make great play of these techniques in their investigations into suspicious deaths. If you don't already know much about this side of police work, you will need to research them. How to go about research is dealt with in Chapter Ten and an Appendix gives details of some books that can be helpful.

Do you have a background in forensics, such as P D James, who worked as a civil servant in the forensics department, or Kathy Reichs, the Canadian crime novelist, who was a pathologist before she became a best-selling author? If so, this can equip you to include fascinating details surrounding the official investigation.

I do not have a scientific mind and I prefer to keep technical details to a minimum. I try to use methods of despatching victims that are relatively simple. For instance, I have used the following:

> Run a victim over with a car. This entailed discovering the car involved and proving that its damaged paintwork matched the traces of paint found on the body.

> Thrown a victim out of a window. This was a very successful crime in that no evidence was left on victim or the site of the crime that could be used to convict the murderer. It also meant that the death was looked on as accidental so that initially there was no murder investigation.

> Attacked a runner on a common with a weighted sock. In this case traces of wool from the sock were found in the wound.

> Used a shotgun at close range. This method necessarily resulted in copious amounts of blood splashing the murderer, who avoided any contamination of their clothes by stripping beforehand and dressing in plastic bin liners. These did not feature in the investigation but could have done. The murderer could have discarded them carelessly and forensics could have been used to identify the victim's blood on the plastic and perhaps a fingerprint of the murderer, maybe a smudged one.

> Electrocution in a kitchen. This method caused me more trouble than any other and proved to my satisfaction that it was better to use simpler ways of killing. A friend gave me details of a wonderfully neat idea that could be used, but my lack of electrical knowledge meant I didn't realise I had made an

elementary mistake in the description. It took an electrical engineer to point it out, and I regret I didn't search one out while I was writing the book and pass a description of the particular method on to them for professional assessment.

➤ Poison. A natural weapon to consider since I was using it in a series of culinary crime novels. The use of poison, however, raises a number of considerations.

Poison as a murder weapon

In an earlier age, authors sometimes relied on a mysterious poison discovered in a South American jungle. It killed instantly and was undetectable. Today's authors have to stick to reality and reality can be difficult when it comes to using poison as a method of murder.

Agatha Christie worked at one stage in a pharmacy and knew a great deal about various poisons. She used this knowledge very effectively in a number of books. However, in the 1920s and 1930s, getting hold of poisons was not particularly difficult. A poison's book was kept by the chemist and it had to be signed by any purchaser. The murderer had to ensure that the signature was not traceable to them. False identities were not difficult to concoct and it's interesting to wonder how many real life victims were despatched without any official investigation being instigated.

Today it is almost impossible for an ordinary member of the public to obtain lethal poisons such as cyanide, arsenic, prussic acid, etc. If such poisons are used in a crime novel, they have generally to be obtained by a member of the medical or some other profession that has legal access to them. Unless administration is very lax, it is not easy even for medics to obtain them, for they will be the first suspects when the loss is identified.

There are, however, a number of poisons occurring naturally in the garden and hedgerow.

Even using these, however, means taking account of the fact that none is the kind of poison that kills instantaneously. Most wreak havoc on the digestive system slowly. *Amanita*

Phalloides, known as the Death Cap Mushroom, takes several days to kill after being ingested. If the poison can be identified in its early stages, antidotes are available (it has to be very early on for *Amanita Phalloides*). The crime novelist, therefore, has to arrange for help not to be available when the victim starts to suffer the usually very unpleasant effects of the poison. I have had to make sure they are alone and unable to call for aid. Or that they do not suspect that they have been poisoned and merely put their unpleasant symptoms down to a nasty stomach upset.

Make sure of details

However you despatch your victims, make sure you are fully aware of the consequences to the body. Also, be quite sure how the killing was done. The majority of murders in crime books are committed off-stage. I always write a description of the death, just as if it was a scene in the book. I can then refer to this every time an investigator theorises about the killing, or evidence is discovered that reveals something about the death. Without this description, it is easy to contradict some detail further on in the book.

Police investigations

Using members of the police force as your main investigators means that they have access to all the forensic information and can interview anyone they feel could be implicated. These two factors are very valuable to the crime novelist and certainly increase the appeal of a police procedural.

The days are gone when the police were regarded as bolt upright members of the community and their characters as being relatively straight-forward. The more modern police novels of Ruth Rendell featuring Detective Inspector Wexford, and those of Reginald Hill with his detectives Daziel and Pascoe, throw much more emphasis on the characters of the policemen, their private lives and how the investigations they are involved with will affect them personally.

Ed McBain, the great American crime writer, wrote a whole series of crime novels around various members of a New York precinct, bringing different officers into the foreground in different books.

A more recent entrant to the crime scene, Simon Kernick, writes gritty, police investigation novels where the difficult task facing modern day police in dealing with organised crime is shown in the way it affects the officers involved. Integrity is constantly called into question; officers are faced with difficult choices when dealing with hardened criminals and do not always remain on the right side of the law.

The crime novelist can make choices between the procedural part of police work and the personal and character-led side. Thanks to a proliferation of television shows featuring police work, both fictional dramas and actual, the public understands very well how a police station operates and how various investigations are conducted. It is not necessary today, therefore, to outline exactly what happens unless it is particularly relevant to the story. As in advertising, a great deal can be sketched in very quickly. Detail should be used to add drama, convey essential information, and illustrate character.

Today's police are seen as much as flawed individuals as any other character in a crime novel. The stresses and strains of their job are reflected in their behaviour. There is a wealth of potential for the crime novelist in police activities but it is as well to understand the basic character requirements for joining the force. An ability to work with other people is important. The maverick who follows their own lines of enquiry and prefers to act on their own is going to find life difficult. Ian Rankin's rightly celebrated Rebus novels beautifully portray the conflicts with authority and petty bureaucracy that a loner can have when pursuing a solitary path in detecting a crime, and how even a gifted detective cannot work entirely alone.

Judith Cutler says: 'All fictional policemen seem to be personally damaged these days: there must be an opening for a well-adjusted, intelligent home-loving cop somewhere on the crime shelves!'

It is also necessary to accept that the police work along designated lines. The discovery of a crime sets in motion established procedures. The investigation follows a routine. To set a novel in this background means understanding what these are.

Exercise

Write up the discovery of a corpse by a young police officer. Describe the procedure that follows the discovery. Imagine that there is a pushy reporter trying to get in on the action. How will the police handle the situation?

How easy did you find this exercise? Did you deal with the trauma experienced by the officer; did you maybe have this as a first encounter with a corpse? Did you describe how the victim had died? Was it obvious a crime had been committed? Did you have the officer contact headquarters? Was the scene secured against contamination?

Other points you might have made would have been to ensure Scenes of Crime Officers were alerted. You might even have had them arrive. Police tape could be erected around the scene, outside if it was al fresco, on the property entrance if the body had been found inside. A route could be established for officials to use to examine the body and the scene to keep contamination of the surrounding area to a minimum.

Don't worry if you found the procedural aspects of the scene difficult. Once you start writing a crime novel, you can always research these (see Chapter Eleven).

By now you should have ideas as to the location and background for your plot, the sort of character your main protagonist and other characters will be, the murder method/s you will use and much more. It is time to start looking at how you will write your book.

Backgrounds & specialist knowledge

> ➢ Set your story in an interesting background world, one you know or can thoroughly research

> ➤ Talk to professionals involved in the world you choose to write about
> ➤ Look for tension and conflict in your chosen background
> ➤ Make sure a series character lives the sort of life that brings them into contact with a wide variety of people
> ➤ If writing a police procedural novel, consider what sort of character becomes a successful member of a police force
> ➤ Decide if there is still a place for the amateur investigator in the modern crime novel
> ➤ Research your chosen murder method/s including forensic details
> ➤ Understand the reactions of everyone connected with the discovery of a corpse

7 Narrative Style and First Paragraphs

It is now time to look at ways of actually writing a successful crime novel; what sort of narrative style you want to use, whether you want to write in the first or third person, and how to start.

Point of view

Before we start, a short explanation of what is meant by 'point of view' may be helpful. POV, as it is often known, refers to the 'eyes' through which the reader is shown what is happening in the book. A character can only see events from their point of view. The author can switch from showing what is going on through one character's eyes to another's, or several others, or can choose to stick to the one. There are many options available and we will look at them all.

Choosing a voice

How are you going to tell your story? Are you going to have a first person narrator, or tell it in the third person?

First person narrator

This can be an attractive way of telling a tale. Read Raymond Chandler and his classic Philip Marlowe books. Read Sue Grafton's Kinsey Milhone novels or Sara Paretsky's V I Warshaski series. These are all books where the character of the narrator infuses the story. They are all Private Investigator books and the reader follows the investigation as the PI unravels the tale. The style is pacey, full of character, and the views of the narrator on what is taking place are expressed with great freedom. The reader is fully engaged with the personality telling the tale and with what is unfolding.

Here is an excerpt from *Farewell My Lovely*, one of the most celebrated of Chandler's books. Philip Marlowe has walked into a fight scene in a bar and met Moose Malloy, who is seeking a girl called Velma. He goes to ask the boss of the bar if he knows her. Having seen Malloy in possession of a gun, Marlowe borrows a sawn-off shotgun from the barman and goes to investigate the boss's office:

> There was a small scarred desk close to a partly boarded-up window. The torso of a man was bolt upright in the chair. The chair had a high back which just reached to the nape of the man's neck. His head was folded over the high back of the chair so that his nose pointed at the boarded-up window. Just folded, like a handkerchief or a hinge.
>
> A drawer of the desk was open at the man's right. Inside it was a newspaper with a smear of oil in the middle. The gun would have come from there. It had probably seemed like a good idea at the time, but the position of Mr Montgomery's head proved that the idea had been wrong.
>
> There was a telephone on the desk. I laid the sawed-off shotgun down and went over to lock the door before I called the police. I felt safer that way and Mr Montgomery didn't seem to mind.

Frank Macshane in his introduction to the Folio Society's collected edition of Chandler's crime novels writes:

> 'It is not easy to have a first person narrator in a detective story, because a great deal must necessarily happen when the detective is not present, which means that tedious explanations may be necessary. But for Chandler, the disadvantage was outweighed by the personality of his character, Philip Marlowe, in whom Chandler was able to instil much of the energy, humour and vitality that he had been unable to bring to ordinary fiction. Marlowe was not Chandler, however. He was a separate entity with a personality of his own. By developing Marlowe's character as fully as he could, Chandler made sure that he was far more than a mere mouthpiece for the author. Indeed, Chandler actually treated Marlowe as though he were a real human being. He would refer to him in his letters as a living person

and comment on his frame of mind and health. To one correspondent,
he wrote a letter of 2500 words describing Marlowe's apartment, his
furniture, his physical appearance, literary preferences, schooling
and taste in drinks, as well as his fondness for chess and his skill in
handling guns. By imagining his character in such detail, Chandler
was able to imbue him with life. Few fictional detectives have been
so meticulously conceived, and the result was an imagined character
of real substance.'

This points up the main drawback to the first person narrator, which is that everything is seen through their eyes. Sometimes great ingenuity is needed to allow the investigator to catch up with events that happen when they aren't present. Without great care, such recapping can become boring. All three of the writers mentioned overcome this limitation in dazzling style, as do many other writers choosing this method of telling their tale.

The fact that the narration is firmly in the control of one person, with everything seen through their eyes, can be turned by the writer into an advantage. Think of Agatha Christie's famous novel, *The Murder of Roger Ackroyd*. The narrator of the story, a doctor, turns out to be the killer of the eponymous victim. At the time of publication, this book caused a sensation. Many readers felt they had been cheated, that they had a right to believe that the narrator would not pull such a dirty trick on them. Since that book, many writers have enjoyed an occasional piece of narrative dexterity in the same vein. The convention that a book written in the first person, or one with the point of view strictly anchored to one character, means that they can be totally relied on has been blown apart.

Reginald Hill's novel *Good Morning, Midnight* opens, as mentioned before, with the suicide of a man restaging the suicide of his father ten years earlier. The victim's preparations for his suicide are complex and intriguing. While baffled as to motive, the reader is made to feel a step ahead of the police. In telling his story, the author intersperses narrative with official statements taken from all the characters involved with either or both suicides, including one from Superintendent Dalziel, who was involved in the investigation of the first. Only at the end of the book can the reader judge how unreliable some of these statements are, but there are sufficient contradictions in the various accounts for alert readers to start questioning what they are being told.

Third person narration

Some authors choose third person narration but confine themselves to the point of view of their main character. For most crime novels, this is the person investigating the crime. This approach can suffer from the same difficulty as first person narration in that events are only seen through one pair of eyes. The narrative is usually less immediate than with the first person but can compensate with a more measured approach and opportunities for more nuances.

Here is an excerpt from *Garnethill*, a novel told entirely from the viewpoint of Maureen, who discovers her lover's knifed body in her living room. This is part of the police interrogation which follows.

> *'Right, Miss O'Donnell. On Thursday you told me that you had never been to the Rainbow Clinic for any kind of treatment, is that correct?'*
>
> *'Yes, I did say that.'*
>
> *'You "did say that". Was it true?'*
>
> *'How do you mean?' she said, fishing for clues.*
>
> *'I think the meaning's quite clear. Did you tell me the truth when you said you hadn't been to the Rainbow for treatment?'*
>
> *Maureen tried to look sad. If she didn't look sorry they'd know she was trying to be clever. She thought about the dream. 'No,' she said, picking it over for the painful element. 'It wasn't true. I lied to you.'*
>
> *'Why did you lie, Miss O'Donnell?'*
>
> *'Because I was ashamed.'*
>
> *'You were ashamed of having an affair with your psychiatrist?'*
>
> *It was being stuck on her back, it was the feeling of being so small and being trapped. She remembered the sensation and her eyes filled up. 'I was ashamed because of the reason I went there.'*

Because this book is seen entirely through Maureen's eyes, the reader is brought to understand and empathise with her and her problems. If, though, it had been written in the first person, Maureen might have come over as less vulnerable and less brave in her fight both to rebuild her life and to uncover the truth behind her lover's death and what she discovers has been happening at the clinic where she has been treated.

There can be other reasons for restricting the viewpoint. Susan Moody's novel *Falling Angel* opens with the main protagonist's discovery of her sister's badly mutilated body. The book is a suspense rather than a crime novel since the actual investigation of the murder, which is assumed to be one of a series of similar murders in the area, is kept very much in the background. Flora, the main character, is concerned with the loss of her sister, the breakdown of her marriage, which occurred before her sister's death, her bitter relations with her mother and the view of motherhood this has given her. Then more deaths occur and Flora has to reassess many of her most cherished beliefs concerning her relationships with those nearest to her. In the process she manages to pick up the clues to the killer that are scattered throughout the book that she (and most readers) had ignored until then. The result is chilling. Had the viewpoint been opened out to include that of other characters, the book would not work in the same way.

Exercise

Write a paragraph or two relating to one of the plots you have worked on earlier that involves your main character. Use the first person. Then rewrite it using the third person.

Can you see a difference in the effect? If so, what is it? Which passage do you think is more effective and why?

Switching point of view

The third person narrative that switches the point of view is the style that gives the author most freedom. It means that the story can be told through the eyes of different people and enables the reader to understand much more about both events and individual characters than if they only saw them through the viewpoint of one person.

Switching viewpoints also means that the reader can be given information not available to the main character.

In John Harvey's *Flesh and Blood*, retired detective, Frank Elder, returns to the case of a vanished teenage girl, Susan Blacklock, when Shane Donald, suspected of Susan's murder, and convicted with another young man of killing another girl, is released from prison after thirteen years.

Frank Elder had promised Susan's mother that he would find her daughter and he'd failed. Now he hopes, finally, to be able to clear up the case. Working unofficially he returns to the Midlands, the scene of the original investigation. Also there are his ex-wife and his teenage daughter. While he is there another girl disappears and once again Shane Donald is suspected.

The story could have been told entirely from Frank's point of view. For the greater part of the book we do see things through his eyes, understand his troubled personal relationships and the powerful effect the case originally had on him. Keeping the narrative solely to his viewpoint would have produced an interesting story but the book is given additional depth and pace by being opened out. It includes scenes from the viewpoint of Shane Donald and that of his probation officer, a female detective who had been on Frank's team, plus others. So the reader is brought to understand something of the suspect, what motivates him and the impact he has on other people. Another advantage of this approach is that, because the reader knows more than Frank does, the suspense of the hunt becomes greater, particularly when Frank's daughter also goes missing.

Sometimes if a scene doesn't seem to be going well, seeing events through a different pair of eyes, switching the point of view in other words, can invigorate the writing and make it more effective.

When using multiple viewpoints, remember that, though your investigator doesn't have to find out everything the reader knows, during the story he needs to acquire sufficient information to solve the central mystery.

Switching viewpoints can be done at any point in the writing. Some authors like to tell one chapter from one viewpoint and then switch to another for the next chapter. Others will change viewpoints within chapters. An indication that this has happened is often given by a break in the text, that is a double spacing sometimes also marked with a star or stars, as follows:

***

This sort of break in the text can also be used to indicate that a certain amount of time has passed, sometimes without the point of view changing.

When switching viewpoint, make the reader aware that this has happened. Introduce the other character by name immediately. This is particularly important if you are not using a break in the text, i.e.:

John placed the gun on the table. He wondered how she would react.

Emma looked at it for a moment then went over to the window. How easily he handled the weapon, she thought.

Now we are absolutely clear that the point of view has shifted from *John* to *Emma*.

Writers used to be advised that the point of view should not shift from one person to another and then back again within a short space of text.

Currently, it is not uncommon to see a rapid change of viewpoint, with the reader first inside one character's head, then in another's, then back again, or onto a third. It can give an effect rather like watching a tennis match.

It almost always gives a more satisfactory read to keep the viewpoint the same for a reasonable stretch of text. This can vary from a page, or even a long paragraph, to a chapter, sometimes several chapters.

Many times it is possible to indicate another person's reactions to a given situation without changing the viewpoint.

For instance, in the brief passage above, if we wanted to stay with John's viewpoint, the text could run:

John put the gun on the table. He wondered how she would react.

Emma looked at it for a moment then went over to the window. 'Where did you learn how to handle a gun?' she said, her back towards him.

Remember that you are the writer; you are the person in control. It is up to you to decide how you want to tell your story and it must be because you feel that it is the right way for that particular book. With another book, you might want to choose a different approach. There is no right way or wrong way, only the way that is your way.

Reginald Hill says, 'What you have to find is the right point of view for your particular plot. You may have to resort to trial and error, but if you are a true creator, you will have no problem recognizing it when at last you chance upon it.'

Show don't tell

Because of the nature of crime novels, almost always there is information that has to be got over to the investigator and the reader. It can sometimes be a temptation to outline this in a straight narrative.

However, it will almost always be more interesting, and more informative, if it is made into a scene.

Exercise

Here is a paragraph describing information that has been obtained by the investigator in a crime story:

As Anne drove to her next appointment, she ran over in her mind what she had learned from Damien Simmonds. It seemed that there was a long-standing feud between him and Andy Marks. There was no way, Damien had said, that he'd spend time with the mechanic unless it was to make sure that he was doing a proper job on his Mercedes. Andy had turned up at his house out of the blue. Anybody who believed that he had invited him round for a drink had to be soft in the head. When Anne had asked Damien why Andy should have made up the story, he blustered and said he had no idea. So, had he invited the mechanic or did Andy have an agenda of his own?

Now rewrite it as an action scene that gets over the same information.

Having done this, do you think the scene is more interesting than the narrative? Have you managed to show more than the information? Here is my attempt:

Anne decided to go and question Andy Marks at his garage.

A large spanner in his hand, the mechanic was bending over what looked like a brand new Mercedes cabriolet. The coachwork was silver, the interior leather a bright red.

'What a fantastic car,' she couldn't help exclaiming. For a moment she had a vision of herself driving it down a fast road, sunglasses on, hair streaming in the wind.

Andy looked up with a sneer. 'Pity the owner doesn't match his motor.' His expression became malevolent. 'Talk of the devil. He can't trust me an inch, can he?'

Anne turned to see Damien Simmonds stride into the garage, his long leather coat swinging open over a black cashmere turtleneck sweater and closely tailored black jeans.

'Ready yet?' he asked curtly.

'Give us a chance! You can't do a full service in five minutes.'

'Don't give me that, it's all done by computers these days, takes seconds. So what you're doing messing around inside my engine, I can't imagine.' His gaze switched to Anne. 'Ah, the little detective, is it? And what are you doing here?'

It wasn't what she had had in mind but the opportunity was too good to miss. 'Good to have you both together,' she said brightly. 'I understand that you asked Mr Marks round to see you the other night, Mr Simmonds.'

'Bollocks. I wouldn't have that piker within half a mile of my place.'

Andy's face reddened. 'You asked me round for a drink, said you had something to discuss with me.'

'Why should I have anything to say to you? You're a nothing. That's what you were at school and have been ever since.'

Andy went white with rage. He raised the spanner he was holding but before he could wield it, Damien grasped his hand.

The two men stood there for a moment motionless, Andy struggling to free his hand, Damien's grip visibly tightening. Then, with a quick twist, he forced the other man to drop the spanner. The mechanic yelped in pain and cradled his injured wrist with his other hand.

'That's a taste of what you'll get if you try to spin stories,' Damien said. 'Make sure that car is ready within the hour.' The leather coat swung again as he strode out of the garage.

This not only gets over the necessary information but fleshes out the characters of Andy and Damien. Now the reader is involved in the conflict between the two men.

Creating an individual style

Writing a crime novel uses all of the same techniques that writing a general novel requires.

One aspect that should be mentioned here is style. The style an author uses is known as his 'voice' and we all have our own, whatever sort of book we write. An author's 'voice' is as personal as their appearance. You've only got to look at the various excerpts given in this book to see how much authors can vary in the way that they write. If you go to the library and study the crime fiction shelves, you will find still more.

Studying the style of other authors can be valuable but there is only one way to achieve your own and that is to write, write, and write. A few people are born being able to put words down in a particular way that is perfect for them. The rest of us have to work at it. The more you write, the more you strive to put into words the story you want to tell in the way you want to tell it, the more personal your style will become.

Write something every day. If you aren't actually writing a book, write about something that has happened to you, the view from your window, or a description of someone you know or have just met. Concentrate on what you want to say rather than how you want to say it, dig down to find the truth of what it is you are writing about. Soon you will find your own voice.

Be ruthless with yourself. Edit all your work. Remove redundant phrases, the repetition of words and those adjectives and adverbs that do little to improve what you are saying. Then look again at your work. Could you have written it more effectively? Approached the piece from a different angle? How much would anyone else be interested in what you have written? Always at the back of a writer's mind there should be a remorseless critic shouting out: Cut that, it's dull. That's far too flowery. You haven't got across what that character's really like. And so on.

First paragraphs

For a first time writer, more than for any other, the most important paragraph in their book is the first.

Krystyna Green, a publishing editor dealing with crime novels says, 'I've now bought at least three novels because of memorable opening paragraphs . . . if I have to struggle with the opening paragraph and the text doesn't pick up after that, then I abandon after Chapter One as if I'm not engaged then chances are no one else will be either – and there is so much competition and talent out there you have to grip your audience from the outset.'

Amongst the many, many submissions Krystyna has had to consider, there was a typescript beginning with thirty pages of solid dialogue – it went straight into the rejection pile.

First paragraphs are vital. It is the first paragraph that potential readers will look at before choosing a book to buy or borrow. If they are not immediately drawn in, they are unlikely to read further. The most brilliant plot is useless it a reader isn't interested enough to read beyond that start on a book.

Even more important, as you can see from that quote above, first paragraphs play a major part in an agent's decision whether to take a book on and an editor's decision as to whether to publish it.

The way a book opens should not only hook a reader and make them want to continue reading; it should also have a flavour of the rest of the book.

Action books usually start with action. A short, violent scene immediately makes the reader want to know what is happening – and what will happen next.

The discovery of a body tells the reader that here is a crime book and how the paragraph unfolds will indicate what sort of a mystery it will be.

An atmospheric first paragraph will suggest a book that will hold the reader's imagination.

A paragraph that sets up a number of questions will intrigue and carry the reader forward to find the answers.

Exercise

Write a first paragraph for a taut, noir crime novel that involves action.

Now write a first paragraph for a 'cosy' crime novel, one that relies on motive and characterisation for its plot rather than violence and bloody descriptions.

Look at your two different paragraphs. Imagine yourself as the reader who has no idea what the book is going to be about (they haven't read the 'blurb', don't know the author).

Do you feel encouraged to read more?

Does the first of your exercises suggest a crime novel that explores the seedy side of life, probably involving lots of action?

Are you intrigued by the paragraph you have written for the second part of the exercise? Are you led to anticipate an enjoyable novel that explores relationships and involves murder and the mystery surrounding murder, but is light on scenes of violence and unpleasant descriptions?

Here are some memorable openings to crime novels:

> The first time I laid eyes on Terry Lennox he was drunk in a Rolls-Royce Silver Wraith outside the terrace of The Dancers. The parking lot attendant had brought the car out and he was still holding the door open because Terry Lennox's left foot was still dangling outside, as if he had forgotten he had one. He had a young-looking face but his hair was bone white. You could tell by his eyes that he was plastered to the hairline, but otherwise he looked like any other nice young guy in a

*dinner jacket who had been spending too much money in a joint that
exists for that purpose and for no other.*

*There was a girl beside him. Her hair was a lovely shade of dark
red and she had a distant smile on her lips and over her shoulders
she had a blue mink that almost made the Rolls-Royce look like
just another automobile. It didn't quite. Nothing can.*

This is that start of *The Long Goodbye* by Raymond Chandler.
To my mind it is the most intriguing of all the openings to his
novels, though *The Big Sleep* runs it close. Everything about
the passage draws the reader in and gives them confidence
that they can trust the author to take them on a roller-coaster
ride that will whisk them into an exciting world combining
mystery and action with cynicism.

*It may be only blackmail, said the man in the taxi hopefully. The
fog was like a saffron blanket soaked in ice-water. It had hung over
London all day and at last was beginning to descend. The sky was
yellow as a duster and the rest was a granular black, overprinted
in grey and lightened by occasional slivers of bright fish colour as a
policeman turned in his wet cape.*

This probably seems familiar because Allingham's description
of the fog was used earlier in this book. However, it's the
combination of the fog with that stunning first sentence
which makes this opening so memorable. If the possibility of
blackmail is 'hopeful', what is the alternative? I defy anyone not
to continue with this book after reading that paragraph.

*You always remember the first time. Isn't that what they say about
sex? How much more true it is of murder. I will never forget a
single delicious moment of that strange and exotic drama. Even
though now, with the benefit of experience and hindsight, I can see
it was an amateurish performance, it still has the power to thrill,
though not any longer to satisfy.*

This is Val McDermid's short opening paragraph to *The
Mermaids Singing,* for which she won the CWA Gold Dagger.
It is breathtaking in how much it tells the reader. It also
offers a warning, if you don't like reading about perverted
serial murders, leave this book alone. However, the skill with

which it is written promises an intelligent and compelling read and few will heed the warning

> *My name is Dodie Blackstock. Well, it's supposed to be Dorothy, but I hate it. And yes, it's those Blackstocks. Wolf Blackstock was my father. I'm the one who inherited all the money. My mother was his third wife. The one who was kidnapped.*

Another short opening but one that promises a very different kind of mystery. This is *Dying Voices* by Laura Wilson. It hooks the reader in with its combination of intriguing information with the raising of questions. Immediately we want to know more about Dodie, her father, all that money, and why her mother was kidnapped.

> *The woman lay on her back on the pebble foreshore at the foot of Houns-tout Cliff, staring at the cloudless sky above, her pale blond hair drying into a frizz of tight curls in the hot sun. A smear of sand across her abdomen gave the impression of wispy clothing, but the brown circles of her nipples and the hair sprouting at her crotch told anyone who cared to look that she was naked. One arm curved languidly around her head while the other rested palm-up on the sea-washed pebbles, the fingers curling in the tiny wavelets that bubbled over them as the tide rose; her legs, opened shamelessly in relaxation, seemed to invite the sun's warmth to penetrate directly into her body.*

Minette Walters starts *The Breaker* with an opening paragraph that combines a descriptive charm with a frankness of approach that is compelling. There are questions that need answering: who is the dead woman, for instance? The description, which infuses her gender with an erotic quality, suggests that sex has had something to do with her death without being in the slightest way pornographic. Finally, how has her body ended up on this deserted-sounding beach?

> *The body lay on a small square of carpet in the middle of the gun-room floor. Alec Chipstead looked around for something to put over it. He unhooked a raincoat from one of the pegs and, covering the body, reflected too late that he would never wear that again.*
>
> *He went outside to see the vet off.*

Here is a beginning that seems to promise one thing, we automatically assume that the corpse on the floor is human, and then, by alluding to the vet, demonstrates that we are wrong. It is the opening of *A Fatal Inversion* by Ruth Rendell writing as Barbara Vine, a book that continues to play with the reader's expectations. Note how the reference to the raincoat never being able to be used again, conjures up a vivid mental picture of what it is to be used to cover, without any need of an actual description. It is also the briefest of character sketches: the man is sensitive but also practical.

Mehmet Ali lay in East London's number one outdoor spot to die. He lay two doors down from Kwame's Hotshot Barbers and three doors up from Rosaman's Cabs. Over him rocked the bodies of two men as they stomped, twisted and sliced their shoe heels into him. An hour earlier his attackers had been jerking their bodies to the pounding energy of Judge Dredd's Nightsound. Now they continued their dance by fucking him up. At first their movements had been light, verbal in nature, with the need to find what they were after. But their tactics had changed once they realised his lips weren't going to tell them anything. After they had found him, as they knew they would, they'd dragged him to Cinnamon Junction, right on to the main road. They had known that this spot was too notorious, too in-your-face, for any of the cars passing on a Monday at 2.23 a.m. to stop and help. Anyway, any car cruising the Junction at that time of morning had its own business to attend to.

This is the start of *Running Hot* by Dreda Say Mitchell, which won the CWA John Creasey Dagger for 2005, the prize which is awarded to the best crime novel by a debut author. It is violent but there is also irony, detachment and an exuberance that promises more than a straight-forward hard-boiled novel.

I've included a variety of first paragraphs not only to illustrate how the reader can be hooked in different ways but also to show, if you hadn't already realised, just how varied crime novels can be. All the above styles are quite different; none could be confused with any other.

Exercise

This is not a quickly done exercise. It could take several weeks but it will be very valuable and should be highly enjoyable.

Go to your local library and spend time assessing openings to crime novels. Take home those books that intrigue you most by their openers, and then read the whole of each. Decide if they fulfil the promise of their opening. How good are the plots? Are the descriptions effective? What about the characterisation? Does the writing drive the story forward? Do the endings satisfy you? Do you want to write this sort of book?

You can admire a novel without wanting to write one like it. You may appreciate the writer's skill without actually enjoying the book. That's fine. What matters is that you learn how you yourself can write the sort of book you want to so effectively that it will attract an agent, a publisher and readers.

Rewriting first paragraphs

Starting a book is difficult. However much time you have spent writing a synopsis, working on character notes and researching background detail, it is writing the book that puts you properly in touch with your characters and plot.

Sometimes the opening paragraph is a way into the book for the writer as well as the reader. Other times it is only when the process of writing is well advanced, maybe even only after it has been completed, that the first paragraph can be satisfactorily written.

It is best, therefore, not to spend too much time worrying about how you have started your book. At any stage you can go back and look at it again. By the time the novel is ready to send to an agent/publisher, though, it should begin in a way that keeps the reader reading.

How literary can a crime novel be?

No crime novel has yet won one of the rich literary prizes such as the Man Booker or the Costa.

Literary critics hold that the crime format (a mystery that requires investigation and a resolution) means crime novels cannot be creative in the same way as they hold literary novels can be. The claim that many contemporary crime novels can be judged by the highest literary standards is made more and more often and the very fact that such a discussion can be held with increasing regularity seems to me to justify these claims. Looking at the standard of many contemporary crime novels, I think it is only a matter of time before one reaches at least the short list of a major literary award. Alex Gray points out that Canongate Books published *The Cutting Room* by Louise Welsh under their mainstream literary label not under the Canongate Crime imprint. It went on to win the CWA John Creasey Dagger.

If a book doesn't work as a general novel, it won't work as a crime novel. The important thing for a crime writer, as for any other fiction writer, is to tell a story in the very best and most effective way possible.

Martin Edwards is one of those who wants crime novels to be classed as literature: 'If a writer can produce wonderful characterisation, a good plot, inventive structure and a grasp of the social mores of the time the novel is set in, he deserves the praise only accorded currently to the literati who seize on it as their due.'

It is now time to look at those essential crime novel techniques such as focus, suspects, clues and red herrings.

Narrative style & first paragraphs

- ➢ Choose first or third person for your novel
- ➢ If choosing the third person, decide whether point of view will be restricted to one person or a number of characters
- ➢ Take care how you switch points of view
- ➢ Show, don't tell – straight forward narrative isn't as effective as a creative scene
- ➢ Writing every day will develop an individual style
- ➢ First paragraphs are vital for drawing in readers and selling your book
- ➢ First paragraphs should give readers a flavour of your book
- ➢ Good crime novels will stand comparison with any 'literary' novel

8 Focus, Suspects, Clues and Red Herrings

A crime novel should have a plot that twists and turns. All but the most alert readers will be seduced into believing one thing, until they are shown by a new twist in the story that matters are very much something else.

Today's successful mysteries have to be more than simply puzzles. They have to operate on every level, characterisation has to be believable, understandable motivation must lie behind every action, dialogue has to work, the narrative has to attract the reader and the story must offer something more than a conundrum to be solved. A crime novel has to be written from the heart just as much as any other novel.

However, with a crime novel the reader expects that a mystery will be unravelled as the book progresses. The unravelling process, though, should be subject to wrong turnings, false starts and information disguised as something else. There may or may not be thrills and spills but the reader will be disappointed if they don't feel challenged to sort out all the tangles along with the investigator, and slightly cheated if the mystery proves too easy to solve. Similarly, if they have not been given all the relevant details needed, buried and wrapped in as many conundrums as the author feels is necessary they will feel cheated.

For both reader and investigator, a crime novel is a journey of discovery.

There is no magic formula for a successful plot. That is up to each individual writer. Ian Rankin says, 'You have to believe you have a story worth telling'.

Changing the focus
or following the trail

Successful crime stories shift the focus of the plot from one situation to another. Details are teased out by the investigator. These sometimes turn out to lead the investigation nowhere useful. More details are then extracted from witnesses, suspects, and others who are involved in the plot in some way.

Writers need to be careful about the number of characters they people their book with. Too many and the reader (not to mention the writer) can get confused. There are writers who helpfully provide a dramatis personae list at the beginning of the book. Others prefer to keep the number of characters, not counting those who appear fleetingly, what might be called 'extras', to what they think the reader can happily retain in their head. Good plots usually start by concentrating on a few characters and then gradually have more added, usually as the focus of the plot shifts.

Shifting the focus is important. The investigation should look like it is heading in a particular direction, only for information to be uncovered or something to happen to cause it to move in another. The plot moves forward along the new path, only to be diverted onto yet another by a further development. The reader should not be allowed to believe they know where the plot is going for too long.

For instance, a crime novel could open with the detective being called in to investigate the discovery of a lorry-load of illegal immigrants. The driver of the truck swears he knew nothing of the load. The detective goes to the trucking company and finds that the managing director has not come in that morning. Then the MD is found dead in his car in a lonely spot with the engine running and a hosepipe leading from the exhaust into the car.

Suicide or murder? The focus has shifted from the illegal immigrants to a suspicious death, but the detective has to investigate whether there is a connection.

The detective tells the victim's wife of her husband's death. She seems very shocked but not all that upset; she assumes it is the result of a traffic accident and asks if his tart was in his car with him. When he hadn't come home the previous night, she'd assumed he was spending the night with his girlfriend.

Now the focus has shifted again. Who is the girlfriend? The wife doesn't know. She is just sure there is one; her husband had been spending too many nights away from home. Could this girlfriend be involved in the illegal immigrant racket?

So the book continues, highlighting first one situation, then another, with both the investigator and the reader uncertain why the man died and where the illegal immigrants fit into the plot, evidence pointing first one way and then another as the detective uncovers more and more information.

I am sure you could work out any number of different solutions to this embryonic plot, plus a number of sub-plots. You could bring in a relationship between the detective and an immigrant he has rescued in the past to underline this aspect of the story. It could turn into a tale of love and loyalty betrayed, as the detective discovers that the wife is having an affair and that the dead man had been about to leave his marriage and his company and retire to Spain with his lover.

Then the lover could turn out to be a man who once drove for the trucking company and organised the illegal immigration racket without the dead man's knowledge. But the dead MD found out and before he could tell the police, the lover murdered him. Or you might dream up something entirely differently.

You would also need a great many more developments and sub-plots. The receptionist in the trucking company could be a legal immigrant from the same country as the illegal ones. She could be a way of informing the reader about the conditions in that country, which make paying over large sums of money for a dangerous journey into the UK seem worthwhile.

The wife of the dead man could be comforted by another director in the firm, and she could start helping to run the company, and so direct energies which haven't been fulfilled by her marriage into a new career which ultimately rebuilds her self-confidence.

Exercise

Outline a murder plot with the focus shifting from suspect to suspect. Take the plot through four different perpetrator possibilities.

Did you find this exercise easy? Splendid if you did, that suggests you have a nimble mind that can exploit different aspects of a plot. If it took a lot of thought, don't worry. Quick and easy solutions aren't always the best ones. Remember the hare and the tortoise. If you find concentrated thinking difficult, go for a walk. There's something about walking that accesses the creative part of the brain.

Shifting the point of view

Shifting the point of view can be an effective way of changing a reader's perspective on the way the story is unfolding.

The brief outline given above could be told entirely as seen through the point of view – through the eyes – of the detective, either in the first or the third person. Or it could be opened out by having various scenes told through the point of view of other characters.

Let's look at another possible plot, one that starts with a detective called in to investigate the murder of a young, pretty girl, called Janine, who has been found one evening strangled in a park.

The detective establishes that the girl had been heard arguing violently with her boyfriend, Paul, who was seen running away from the park shortly before the body was discovered by a friend who was staying with the victim at her flat very near to the park. The friend, let's call her Delia, had gone out on a date and discovered the body on her way home. She immediately called the police on her mobile.

On being questioned, Paul denies having had anything to do with Janine's death. He says he didn't even see her that evening; the witness must have confused him with another man. But it turns out that Paul had previously been arrested for assault, although the victim had changed her mind about bringing a charge against him.

So far the story is being written from the detective's point of view and he and the reader have every reason to suspect that the boyfriend, Paul, strangled Janine to death in a momentary rage.

Now the reader can be given a passage written from the point of view of Delia, Janine's girl friend. This could reveal that Delia is actually pleased that Janine is dead, they weren't such close friends as she'd told the detective, in fact Janine had seduced Delia's boyfriend. Delia had pretended not to mind but in fact has been waiting for an opportunity to revenge herself on Janine.

This passage could be written in such a way as to suggest without actually stating it that Delia murdered Janine. As far as the reader is concerned, a great big question has been raised. In fact, two questions: what was Delia's part in Janine's death, and exactly what sort of girl was Janine? There could also be the possibility that Paul was the boyfriend Janine had seduced.

Readers have now not only become aware that the background to the murder is more complicated than it first appeared, they are in possession of information that so far the investigator doesn't have. This can give the reader a comfortable feeling that they are ahead of the detective.

It's up to the author to decide how long it should be before the detective finds out about Delia's possible involvement in Janine's death and where the suspicion should next fall. Is there another boyfriend? Has Janine been involved with a married man and threatened to tell his wife about their affair? Or has the wife found out? As the story unfolds, all these characters can be given passages told from their point of view. This helps shift the focus and also deepens the background to the story, which could be all about love and loyalty.

The more information the reader is given about the characters, the more interested they will be in them.

Another advantage in being able to switch the point of view is that it is easier to alter the pace of the story by moving it away from the principal character or characters. For more on pace, see Chapter Nine.

Voices from the grave

It is difficult for a murder victim to speak for themselves. In my crime books, I prefer not to dispatch a victim until they have appeared in the book. This enables the reader to have some idea of their character and perhaps why someone should want to murder them. Readers must be made to feel emotions.

Peter Lovesey's book, *Diamond Dust*, opens with a brief court scene with a guilty verdict on a criminal that Peter Diamond, Lovesey's contemporary series detective, has been responsible for putting in prison. There follows a short scene outside the court when Diamond is attacked by the angry mistress of the guilty man, who she swears is innocent. There is then an elegiac scene with Diamond at home. While his wife, Stephanie, attends to the scratches on his face, he fills in the details on the case and explains why the man couldn't possibly be innocent. This scene does a double duty. It gives the reader essential information and also shows the deep happiness of their twenty year old marriage. In the next chapter, Diamond is called to a shooting scene and finds when he gets there that the victim is his wife.

Lovesey has enabled the reader to feel Diamond's terrible pain and made it quite clear that Diamond himself could not possibly have been involved in her killing. This is important a little later as Diamond finds that, as far as the police investigation is concerned, he is the chief suspect. The reader, at least, is certain he can't be the killer.

Opening a book with a dead body that the reader knows nothing about, though, can be very effective. The investigation can then reveal different sides of the victim's personality and life, each new revelation causing a rethink about the identity of the murderer.

One of the ways that victims can be allowed to speak for themselves is for the author to insert passages from a diary or a series of notes or letters. Very often in the book these are printed in italics to show that the passages are not part of the ongoing investigation.

Exercise

Look again at the brief notes on the murder of Janine given above and write a passage from her diary in which she says she hates someone and knows how she can give them their comeuppance. Do not identify the person or exactly what she intends to do. But give a flavour of what sort of girl Jessica is. I would probably write something like the following:

Tuesday: I was in the middle of a dreadful report – I'm definitely going to look for another job – when the phone rang. Another appeal for me to stop. I'd rather eat dog turds – and how sick is that! Are they stupid or what! I said by the time I'd finished, no one, but no one, would even say hello to them. What is it they say about revenge being sweet? I'll say it is.

Nothing about this passage identifies in any way who it is making the appeal to Janine. However, it is quite clear that Janine has threatened the caller in some way and that she has information that could be very damaging to them. It also suggests that Janine is not a very nice person. Another excerpt from the diary later on could show a more attractive side, or not, as the author wishes.

Voices within

This same technique can be used for anonymous passages. These, too, are often printed in italics. Such passages are particularly effective when used to demonstrate how disturbed that character is; the opening of Val McDermid's *The Mermaids Singing* quoted earlier is a case in point. The passages may reveal sinister intent. They may alert the reader (but not the detective) to murder or murders to come and so increase the suspense.

The passages can be written in such a way that the reader feels sure they have identified who is writing them, only to find later on that the actual author is someone else. Or the reader may be left entirely in the dark.

Such passages can be very atmospheric, can throw doubt on conclusions suggested by the main text, or create suspense by suggesting some horror that is to come. Susan Moody uses this technique very effectively in *The Italian Garden,* a book that is full of atmosphere and suspense.

As with switching points of view, such passages can give the reader information that may not be available to the investigator.

It is a convention, though, one that any author of a crime novel breaks at their peril, that the investigator should never be in possession of information which is denied to the reader. It is just about permissible to hold up the revelation or piece of critical evidence for a chapter or so to increase reader suspense, but not for longer.

Number of suspects

This is a good point at which to talk about how many suspects a crime novel should have. Much will depend on your story and the number of characters you want to write about. Remember that if you have too many, the reader will get confused. If you have too few, though, it will take considerable skill to keep the reader mystified as to which character committed the crime. I've already mentioned that Minette Walters in her book *The Breaker* very skilfully limits the number of murder suspects to three and shows how a clever writer can keep the reader enthralled.

Most writers will include not less than three suspects but rarely more than six.

Reginald Hill's entertaining *Good Morning, Midnight,* though, has many more. It starts with a chapter set in 1991 at the end of the first Gulf War with the discovery by a young boy in Iraq, the Middle East, of the body of a black girl in a packing case. He unintentionally sets off an unexploded bomb, whose blast he just escapes. Then we shift to 2002 and the suicide mentioned earlier where a son replicates the way his father's death was staged. The police investigation involving Reginald Hill's regular detectives, Andy Daziel and Peter Pascoe, has to reopen the previous incident as well as try to decide whether this death was a suicide or a cunning, locked room murder. The story switches rapidly from character to character, the current action and the past cunningly interwoven, the point of view moving from police to suspects, to non-suspects. The relationships between the various participants unfolds brilliantly as the story progresses. Reginald Hill's crime novels are beautifully twisty and he is a master of language. *Good Morning, Midnight* marries great subtlety of characterisation with an understanding of how world events can impinge on lives seemingly uninvolved with them. It ends with a scene in Iraq after the invasion when another body is discovered, neatly tying up a loose end from the main story. Like others in the Dalziel and Pascoe series, the book is a lesson in how a complicated story can be told without confusing the reader and how it can keep readers turning the pages. Reginald Hill's prose is a constant delight.

Exercise

Read a whodunit crime novel and make notes of how the focus of the story is switched from character to character. Decide how successful the author has been in the use of voice/s and the point of view. Note the number of suspects. Finally, decide how interested you were in the story. If you were enthralled, what kept you that way? If you feel the author failed to keep your interest, work out why.

Note also how the story was told, whether in the first person or the third. If in the third, was it told from one point of view or several? How satisfying did you find the choice the author made in the way the story was told?

Series character

Publishers like series novels. A series character builds reader loyalty. If they enjoy the first novel, they will want to read the second and then the third. Hopefully there will be enough readers to convince the publisher to keep buying the books.

A great deal of thought needs to go into the creation of a series character. They have to be someone you will enjoy writing about for many books, which, as mentioned earlier, means also that they have to be involved in the sort of work that can bring them into contact with a variety of corpses. Readers will have to be involved in their story just as much as with the characters they meet in the course of their investigations. That means you have to choose their background very carefully. An obvious choice is a policeman or a private eye, but there are many other professions where your series character could become involved with an investigation, some of which were mentioned in a previous chapter.

Remember that whatever characteristics or background you give to your series character, they will have to remain with them through however many books you write featuring them. Think about ageing. Are you going to have them grow in real time or, like Sue Grafton, gradually allow them to work in a period ten, fifteen or even twenty years earlier than the one you are writing in? Or are you going to fudge and slow the ageing process but keep the writing contemporary? Are you going to move them about the country, or the world, or keep them in more or less the same surroundings?

John Malcolm's advice is, 'If you are writing a series, retain the salient characters and background from book to book, but change everything else as much as possible.'

Judith Cutler says, 'I have to enjoy being in the head of my protagonist. I may not necessarily like or even admire whoever this is, but he or she has to intrigue me, so I can spend many hours in their company and still want to switch on the computer the following day knowing I shan't be bored.'

Clues

Clues can be seen as ways of indicating aspects of the story are not what they seem. The more subtle they are, the more successfully they can reveal the truth only to the sharpest investigators and readers. Martin Edwards says, 'My favourite novels are character driven, rather than plot driven. Clues there must be, but I prefer to use them as an orienteer uses points he must visit: vital but not necessarily the point of the novel as a whole.'

Just as the police investigate a crime and build up a picture of what has happened, amassing pieces of evidence and details of the suspects involved, so does the novelist and the reader. Sometimes 'whodunnit' is only revealed to both investigator as well as the reader in the very last pages of the book.

However, the account that is given to the reader must contain enough pieces of background information to make the unmasking plausible. These clues should be available to both investigator and reader. Sometimes, though, the information can be so subtly conveyed that only the alert reader will draw the same conclusion as the investigator.

Clues of inference

One of my favourite 'clues of inference' is in Dorothy Sayers' *Five Red Herrings*. Early on in the book there is a scene with a painting on an easel in the countryside, the inference being that the artist has abandoned it. There is a description of the painting. Lord Peter Wimsey (Sayers' skilful amateur detective) lists the paints found at the scene. Though the painting includes clouds, there is an absence of white paint. This is not pointed out and it takes an alert reader to realise that this means the scene has been created as an elaborate device to throw an investigation off the scent.

Dorothy Sayers is very skilful at planting these clues. In another book, *Gaudy Night*, when investigating a crime scene at an Oxford college, Peter Wimsey examines a door and congratulates the Dean on how well her college is cleaned. Only later is it pointed out that the fact that the top of a door had been wiped free of dust was relevant to the investigation.

John Harvey in *Flesh and Blood* has his retired detective, Frank Elder, re-examining witnesses in an attempt to establish exactly what happened to a teenager who'd disappeared thirteen years earlier. It was assumed Susan Blacklock, the teenager, was a victim of a sadistic duo who had killed at least one other girl. A witness tells Elder that Susan had fallen out with her dad; she had heard them going at each other hammer and tongs:

'Crying she was and telling him to leave her alone. "You got no right to talk to me that way. No right." And him coming back to her, "Yes, I have. As long as you're under my roof, I've every right." I don't know what it were about, something she should or shouldn't have done, I dare say. In the end she run off …'

Elder doesn't draw any conclusions from this piece of evidence. It is only much later in the book that he learns from another witness that Susan had been adopted; a fact the investigation at the time had been unaware of. Any step-parent is familiar with the cry, *'you have no right …'* from a step-child but even they may fail to recognise it here. Throughout the book, readers have to re-assess relations and events.

Clues in lists

Another way of burying a clue is in a list or a description, which readers tend to skip over. An account of the contents of a handbag or an office drawer could have in it something that later becomes relevant. Robert Wilson used this technique in *A Small Death in Lisbon*.

After a great deal of trouble, the police have been able to trace the movements of the murdered teenage girl during the afternoon of her death. They find a witness who saw her get into a car, a black Mercedes with tinted windows. So then the hunt is on for more information about the car. The two detectives heading the investigation work the bus queues where the car had been seen, showing a photograph of the dead girl and trying to find a witness who saw her get into the car so they could provide a better identification of the vehicle.

'It was an advertisement for not committing crime because there's always somebody out there who's seen you. Four people saw Catarina get into the black Mercedes. One guy remembered it like it was one of the best scenes from his favourite movie. The car in front was a metallic grey Fiat Punto. The black Mercedes was a C200 series, petrol engine with the letter NT in the registration. The car behind it was an old white Renault 12 with a rusted rear wheel-arch.

*And the car that Jamie Gallacher fell against was . . . I told him that
he'd given us more than we needed and took his name.'*

Now the detectives have enough information to enable
them to find the Mercedes and arrest the man whose car the
murdered girl entered that afternoon. He is brought to court
and convicted of murder. Much, much later in the book,
comes this passage between the two detectives as they idly
take in a white van and discuss what they feel they missed
in the case:

*'It's nice to see one of those still running,' said Carlos.
'And now, finally, you start talking about cars,' I said.
'That,' said Carlos, 'is a Renault 12. Car of the Year back in the
1980s sometime. My father had one ... but his was a pile of shit.
I spent a lot of my youth working on one of those.'
The two ventricles of my heart iced up. Suddenly the blood was
only going through in thin spurts and the oxygen in my breathing
hard to find.*

Coelho has remembered the description of the Mercedes,
how the car had been followed by an old white Renault 12
with a rusted wheel arch. Both detectives had completely
overlooked the possibility that someone might have been
following the man in the Mercedes. It is this that leads them
to the conclusion that the wrong person might have been
convicted for the murder.

Two-way clues

A way of deflecting a reader's attention away from a clue is
to make it achieve two different aims. For instance, you want
to show a couple having an argument, trying to score off
each other during a luncheon party. You could have the man
complaining about the woman's driving:

'Who never uses fifth gear, eh? And is always in the wrong
queue?'

'You sicken me. It wasn't you, I suppose, who got stuck
for two hours in Nice last summer?'

'Is a traffic jam my fault? And that's nothing to the way you never, ever, overtake when the road is clear for miles.'

'You really are a bastard. You're the one who got stopped for dangerous driving.'

'That cop was the biggest wanker. Couldn't understand I like to be in front of idiots on the road rather than behind them. I'd hate to be behind you.'

The author hopes that the reader will let the reference to a traffic jam in Nice pass them by because it is the relationship between the couple that is the main interest. Later, the man is suspected of forming a relationship with a murder victim the previous summer in Nice. He denies having been there then and is backed up by his wife. Because of their difficult relationship, the wife's evidence is given weight. Will readers remember the reference to Nice during that lunch?

Two-part clues

Clues can be divided into two parts, each set in the book at a distance from one another. They can reveal a character to be other than what they have claimed to be. Take someone who applies for a job with a CV stating that they have a degree in English. Much, much later on in the book, the character is visited in their home and the description reveals, without making a point of it, that there are no books in the living room. What English graduate exists without books?

Red herrings

Red herrings are clues that point the reader in the wrong direction. They operate in exactly the same way as other clues but are left just a little more obvious.

For instance, take the arguing couple I created above. The investigator is trying to discover which character was in Nice the previous summer. There could be a passage in which an old-fashioned kitchen drawer is jerked out too far by a nervous suspect and falls to the floor. In the description of its contents as they are picked up there could be a receipted invoice from the Hotel Negresco on the Promenade des Anglais, Nice. The reader can feel pleased at picking up the suggestion that here is someone who was there at the right time.

Exercise

Take a plot you have been working on and create two clues, one which will point your investigator towards the actual killer and one which will be a red herring. Make notes on how both clues can be incorporated into your book.

Now that we have dealt with various crime novel techniques, it is time to look at the pace of your book.

Focus, suspects, clues & red herrings

> ➤ The focus of plots should shift direction as the book unfolds, introducing new characters and possible motives

> ➤ The true nature of characters, including corpses, should be gradually revealed

> ➤ Create enough suspects for the perpetrator not to be obvious but not so many that the reader becomes confused

> ➤ Think carefully about choosing a series character, their profession, how they will get involved with various crimes, possibilities for character development over a number of books

> ➤ Provide enough clues for the alert reader to solve the mystery but bury them in the story and make red herrings slightly more obvious

> ➤ Study how leading crime books achieve their effects

Pace or
The Smoking Gun

This chapter is all about keeping the reader reading.

Alex Gray says, 'Critics of the genre may protest that it is all formulaic but I believe that good crime writing needs to be highly thought out and structured. It is vital to keep several strands of storyline going at once in order to tease the reader and keep the pace of the story going as well as to provide mini cliff-hangers along the way. This is not as simple as it may sound. All sorts of demands are made on the writer of crime fiction including planting red herrings, giving credence to a variety of motivations and providing enough action for the plot. I've often heard crime writers talking flippantly about throwing in another body if the narrative seems to be flagging, but there is an awful lot more to keeping suspense and interest going for the reader than that.'

Questions

So much about writing a successful crime novel is concerned with questions.

When introducing a character, don't tell the reader everything about them immediately. In fact, tell as little as seems necessary. No, tell them less than is necessary but make it intriguing. If readers have questions, if they want to know more, they will keep reading.

Never give the reader a comprehensive account of an event. Leave questions to be answered later. In a police investigation, a crime scene always raises questions and so it has to be with a crime novel. It is like a pie, we want to know what is under the crust. If an aroma wafts out of it, we can tell if it will be a meat, fish or apple pie but not much more about its contents. Even after the pie is cut and a piece laid on the plate, we may still not know everything about it, how it has been seasoned, whether it contains spices or what the curious-looking dark bits are.

A book, even a short one, takes time to read. The author needs to keep the questions coming. Certain questions will be answered but more will be raised. The last piece of information the reader requires should be on the last page. Sometimes a book can end with yet another question.

Natasha Cooper says, 'Keep up the tension. You have to give readers a reason to stick with you until the end of your novel. To do this you will need to make them like at least one character so much that they care what happens. You will also need to plant questions in their minds and delay providing the answers. The answer can be anything from the most obvious – will the woman tied to the railway line be rescued before the express train mashes her to a pulp? – to the emotionally subtle, eg.: will the sleuth be able to control her own instinct to keep everyone happy in time to use what she knows to expose the person who is protecting the vicious killer?'

Chapter hooks

The danger point, the time when a book can lose a reader, is at the end of a chapter. They decide that they'll read to the natural break, then take the dog for a walk, or make supper, or put out the light.

The end of a chapter usually signals the end of a particular part of the story. Like the conclusion to a movement in a symphony, it often conveys a natural fall in the way that the story is being told. We use the cliché about our lives: one chapter is ending, another is about to begin, because it is so true.

The way to avoid the reader closing the book, maybe never to open it again, is to have a 'hook', something that drags them onto the next chapter and keeps them reading.

Here are a number of hooks that the author can use:

> You can leave a character in extreme danger at the end of a chapter – and then start the next chapter with a different location and another set of characters, leaving the one that is in danger until later to be rescued – or to succumb to disaster.

> A character can be faced with a decision that has to be made – in the next chapter or the one after that.
> Danger can be seen approaching – not to be resolved until a future chapter.
> A development of some kind is signalled.
> A provocative statement is made that needs a reaction – which it won't receive until the next chapter.
> The chapter is shaped in such a way that the reader has to follow the action, even though it continues into the next chapter.

All of these are 'hooks' that can drag the reader onto the next chapter.

Exercise

Take a crime book that you admire, and look at the end of each chapter. How has the author ensured that you will want to read on to the next?

Do keep remembering 'hooks' when you come to the end of a chapter. Don't let the reader find it easy to close the book and do something other than keep turning the pages.

Pace

You have your opening paragraph, your cast of characters, as much idea of what is to happen as is necessary for your writing methods, whether it is a full-blown scenario, a few pages, or just the opening idea. You are starting to unravel the mystery that is going to be put before the reader. You know about asking questions, changing the focus, not revealing everything at once about your characters and what is happening, and about hooks at the end of chapters. You now have to remember pace.

In a way, writing a book is like conducting an orchestra. Instruments need to be brought in at the correct time, themes and variations have to be displayed, each development of the music has to be brought to the audience's attention. And the conductor has to make sure that the piece the orchestra is playing is given its proper shape, that the music drives on in a satisfying way to its conclusion. This is what pace is all about.

It is difficult to give rules for pace, so much of it is dictated by what could be termed as the author's internal clock. This is something inside a writer that constantly monitors how the book is progressing and determines the introduction of new characters, where the next scene is to be set, when action should be introduced, when to draw out a scene, when to use shock tactics. These aren't always got right in the first draft but faults should be identified and corrected in the second and, maybe, further drafts.

A crime book should never be a leisurely exploration of plot and character. It should be constantly on the move. If you were to draw a graph reflecting the pace of a successful book, it would be a series of rising curves. A peak of tension would be followed by a slight relaxation, perhaps a diversion of some sort that will hold the reader's attention but not in the same way, then the action tightens again to another peak, a little higher than the earlier one, and so on, with the overall pace quickening until final drama of the denouement.

Here is Reginald Hill's definition of pace. 'Pace doesn't mean speed, it means the right speed. Diagnosis and cure are simple. If you've reached where you want to be too quickly, ask yourself what you've missed out. If too slowly, ask what took you so long.' He calls also for something he classifies as continuity: 'What I mean by the term is wholeness, hanging-togetherness, integrity, dynamism. It's the quality which makes you reluctant to break off reading even though you know you ought to be cutting the lawn or picking your kids up at the station or saving the world from alien invasion. It's difficult to define, but like a cold in the head, if you've got it, you'll know it.'

Characterisation, atmosphere, metaphor, all the tools of a writer's trade have to be employed as effectively as possible, but most important of all, is the need to drive the plot along.

As I write a book, I try to see a scene with the eye of the reader. I ask myself:

- ➢ Am I interested?
- ➢ Does the scene tell me more about the plot and the characters?
- ➢ Have I expressed what is there in as interesting a way as I can?
- ➢ Are there any clichés? (If there are, get rid of them; find a different way to express what you want to say that is fresher and more appealing.)
- ➢ Have I used too many words?
- ➢ Does there need to be a change of pace anywhere?

Here's some more advice from Natasha Cooper: 'Vary the emotional intensity. People cannot live in a state of unremitting drama, and any novel that suggests they can loses credibility. Intersperse action scenes with reflective ones and never forget that one emotion intensifies its opposite, ie: if you're about to plunge your readers into tragedy it will be more effective if you've softened them up with humour or gentle emotion in the preceding scene.'

Technicalities are important but they have their own inbuilt danger. Sarah Turner, a leading editor, says, 'The crime novelist must pay so much attention to form, plot and pace that the true meat of the novel can find itself squeezed out altogether. The sense of place, the sense of period, the peripheral characters – the elements that lift the words from the page – are every bit as important as the mechanics. Suspense reaches boiling point only when we are invited deep into the novel's atmosphere.'

Andrew Taylor, the award-winning crime writer, says 'Less is more'. This dictum can be applied to every facet of writing.

Less is more

There are leisurely writers who can express themselves superbly, can write a description using beautifully chosen phrases and figures of speech, can dig inside a character and reveal as vital a human being as you could meet in the real world, but sometimes their work would have been more effective if it had undergone a ruthless editing pen.

Writing effectively usually means using fewer words. Avoid repetition. Make descriptions sharp rather than lengthy. Be wary of long sentences; you will probably express what you want to say better in two or even three much shorter sentences.

Watch paragraphs. As soon as the point for that paragraph has been made, move onto another one.

Check whether you need to describe how a character has uttered a phrase or sentence. As long as the reader is not confused as to who is speaking, dialogue usually runs best uninterrupted by 'he said', 'she gasped', 'he sighed', etc, etc.

The shorter the sentences, the more the pace of a story picks up. In a tense scene in *The Long Goodbye* between Marlowe and a brutal detective, Chandler describes the policeman's reaction to a typically unco-operative Marlowe remark as follows:

His jaw muscles bulged. His eyes were dirty ice. 'So?'

No need for, 'he grunted', or 'he gritted', or 'he barked' to be added. Everything necessary is in those two sentences before the one word, 'So?'

Exercise

Locate a creative piece you wrote for a previous exercise. Try to find quite a long one. Now read it through and edit it to make it more effective. Adverbs and adjectives are often redundant and slow down pace. Check for repetition, both ideas and words, and unnecessary descriptive phrases. Remember, though, that you are not doing a school précis. You must retain the atmosphere you created but heighten it by making it sharper. Make every word count.

Polishing a first draft can be very satisfying. The ideas are there and it is usually getting ideas down on paper that is the most difficult job; making sure those ideas are expressed more effectively is easier. Some writers polish each page as they write so that when they reach the end of the book, it is ready to be sent off. These writers almost always work with a detailed scenario. Other writers complete a first draft and then go back and polish. Often they have to include further material that will foreshadow events they hadn't realised would occur. Sometimes a particular approach, such as using the first person, for instance, is changed for another and the whole book has to be rewritten.

Ann Granger used seven drafts for one of her books. '*Shades of Murder* has a plot which takes place in two time zones, one Victorian and one modern and moves back and forth. After first writing it like that, I had a change of mind and rewrote it, putting the whole thing in the present and ditching the Victorian bits. Then I changed my mind once more and rewrote again, putting the Victorian chapters back, but approaching them in a slightly different way. Then one of the minor characters turned out to be more interesting than I'd first thought so I expanded her role.'

Reducing exposition

There are times when a writer has to get over information to the reader but actually wants to get on with writing the next bit of the story. The information bit feels boring but the author keeps on writing it because it has to be there, doesn't it? If the author feels bored by part of their book, don't you think the reader will be as well?

Any time that even a hint of having to get over information makes you yawn, stop writing. Take a look at what you have to tell the reader and think of a better way of getting it across. Can you involve another character, make the giving of information reveal a side of someone that has not been explored until now? Can you create tension out of the telling? Can you slip in the information via a conversation in a gripping situation? Perhaps your detective/investigator and a companion can have a conversation getting over the vital details while they are investigating another aspect of the case. Intrigue the reader as well as informing them.

On the other hand, never forget that stating a fact quickly and simply can often be very effective: 'Tennant skimmed quickly through the medical jargon of the post mortem report. There was only one detail he hadn't known already. The victim had been pregnant.'

Skipping over time

Unless you are writing a version of *Twenty Four Hours,* or even if you are, it should not be necessary to go through every detail of a day or an investigation. Time passing can easily be summed up: 'It was three days later and the investigation had got nowhere. Then the telephone rang.'

Often you don't even need that. Today's readers have been educated through television to accept sharp editing of scenes and can follow changes that occur without explanation. They can fill in the links themselves.

Your reader has to believe that the story is always going forward. We know that life isn't like that and there can be long periods when nothing very much happens but a book can't afford to wallow in inertia.

Peter Lovesey finds that the most difficult scenes he has to write are, 'the links, when I've finished a key chapter with all its excitement and have to move on and explain what other characters were doing meanwhile'.

What he enjoys most is, 'When my readers and I know what's going on and those poor benighted characters are unaware of what they're walking into.'

However, there are ways of making capital out of sticky patches. Perhaps for the sake of your story there has to be a week's gap, say, between one event and another. You want to show your main protagonist frustrated at the lack of action. Rather than skip lightly over that week as above, you could have a scene that reveals another side of your character:

Until the test results came through the following week, there was little I could do. I decided it was too long since I'd visited my parents. A few days listening to Dad pontificate on the state of the nation would no doubt drive me nuts but Mum's food would be a bonus and there was always the beach. Walking along the sand, watching waves do what waves do, listening to the seagulls, even in winter, had always helped me sort out problems. And my current problems needed some sorting.

I got the welcome that always made me wonder why I didn't come down more often. Then Dad got stuck into the whisky and what a disaster the present government was and I knew why. But over dinner, roast beef with Yorkshire pudding like no one else makes it, Mum said suddenly, 'Jan's back. Why don't you give her a ring?'

I almost choked on my third helping. 'What happened? Lover boy not up to it?'

Jan and I had once been an item. Then a New York thruster had invaded my territory and for two years Jan had been living in the Big Apple. Now, according to Mum, she was home again. I thought of the laughter in the eyes I could never decide were green or grey, the sway as she walked that could always raise my blood pressure; then I pushed the memories away. Jan was a complication I needed like a recovering alcoholic needs a dry martini.

'I've asked her to dinner tomorrow night,' added my dearly-loved mother.

It's never a good idea to get too far away from the main story line, but a sub-plot that involves your chief protagonist, and which can be dove-tailed into, or run in counter-point to, the prime investigation, can deepen the reader's involvement.

Opening with a bang

We have agreed, I hope, that opening paragraphs have to hook the reader. Now let's look at what that opening should lead into.

Conflict is what drives a plot. The reader needs to know early on how the conflict in this particular story will arise. You may feel you need to start your book with some cosy scenes, showing how idyllic life was for certain of your characters before disaster struck. Most of us want happiness and contentment in our lives, but that's not what we read books for. Have more than one short scene that's all sweetness and light and you run the risk of reader-boredom.

Think about having the disaster strike first and then a flashback showing what has been destroyed. The reader will wince at the contrast and be instantly involved in the story.

They will want to know what happens next to these tortured souls.

I've already mentioned Peter Lovesey's *Diamond Dust*. He had to show the reader how happy his detective, Peter Diamond, was with his wife before she was murdered but solved the problem by opening his book with a court scene followed by an action scene before the scene with his wife.

Characters have to be set in conflict with other characters. The crime investigation has to uncover incidents that cause trouble for those involved. It can help the story if your investigator is involved with a personal conflict or dilemma. However, this must not be allowed to slow the pace of the story.

Continuing with fireworks

Around the middle of a novel, with the main excitement having taken place and the investigation now proceeding, writers sometimes find it difficult to maintain momentum.

Raymond Chandler's maxim was, if you need to up the excitement factor, bring in a man with a gun.

Not so easy these days, even if guns are easier to get hold of than most of us would like. If you are writing a crime novel that isn't centred on a gangland culture, it would probably be inappropriate.

However, the basic idea behind Chandler's maxim can work in other ways. An investigation can be kept interesting by the introduction of another murder. Often the second corpse is that of the character who up until then has been the main suspect. This forces the reader to reassess the situation and try to work out who has done both murders (there are plots that have more than one killer but, as a general rule, it is more satisfactory to stick to one murderer).

There is also the possibility of introducing threats to the life of the main protagonist, increasing the suspense element of your plot.

When considering the development of your story, consider its momentum carefully, bearing in mind that you have to keep your reader riveted. The pages must be kept turning, while remembering that the book must also have an overall shape.

Bringing your book to a conclusion is something that needs careful consideration and that is what the next chapter is concerned with.

Pace or the smoking gun

> ➢ Keep the reading wanting answers to questions
> ➢ End each chapter with a 'hook' to draw readers onto the next
> ➢ Don't allow the technicalities of telling a story to interfere with its atmosphere
> ➢ Begin with conflict and tension and introduce new elements to keep the story alive
> ➢ Keep asking yourself as you write if the story is interesting
> ➢ Reduce exposition and keep linking passages to a minimum
> ➢ Always edit your work tightly and remember that less is more

10 Denouements and Endings

Most writing advice concentrates more on beginnings than endings. And it's easy to understand why. Get the beginning right, get characterisation, development of plot, dialogue and everything else right and the ending should follow. I said earlier that I never know how the book I'm about to embark on will end – until I get to the point when I have to write it.

Some writers conceive the end of a book at the same time as the beginning. I've met writers who have known what the last line of their book has to be at the time they write the first. Many more of us, though, work towards those magic words THE END trusting that all will in due course become clear.

When reaching the end of a crime book, it is sometimes tempting to allow the criminal to escape arrest. However heinous the crime, getting inside the perpetrator's head and understanding their motivations, can generate admiration, and perhaps even affection, and thus a wish to organise some form of escape for them. Patricia Highsmith's Ripley is the most famous case of a writer producing crime novels from the point of view of the criminal, who, at the end of the book, has, like an eel, escaped his proper desserts. A highly intelligent and clever writer, Highsmith pulls it off but, for most crime writers, it is a dangerous example to follow.

In a piece on *The Psychology of Crime Writing*, Alex Gray has looked at the necessity of seeing that justice is done at the end of a crime book:

'Recent statistics show that Strathclyde Police have a success rate of 98.6% in solving murder cases, a statistic that is mirrored in fiction. A crime novel where the perpetrator successfully carried out his crime and denied the reader any real satisfaction is, in my opinion, far less successful, psychologically speaking, than one where the outcome was in favour of the detective and/or the victim of the crime.

Even when one of Dame Agatha Christie's murderers escaped from his opponents, she made sure that they met with a fatal ending in one way or another, suggesting that even an accidental death was justice meted out by the Fates who also seem to care about the psychology of crime fiction!

The exceptions to this rule are those crime series where the criminal lives to fight another day and to present an ever-present danger to the protagonist. The American crime novelist, Patricia Cornwell, is one writer who makes use of this device. However, I believe that the reader desires a sense of relief at the conclusion of a piece of crime fiction and a sense that justice has been meted out. In the real world we are made aware of murder investigations by following stories in the Press, watching news items or TV programmes such as the BBC's Crimewatch UK, where it sometimes takes months or even years before a perpetrator is brought to justice. Within the covers of our novels we are able to give the reader much more immediate satisfaction, especially if we create a real page-turner.'

We all know that life is unfair. Many people who deserve success do not achieve it. The good die young, the rotters get away with their crimes. Readers, though, want realism but also a sense of justice. If you really do want your criminal to get away with anything, make sure that the reader does too by offering the sort of extenuating circumstances that will ensure sympathy. The badly beaten wife who finally turns on her bully of a husband is an obvious example.

Whatever the ending of your novel, there are certain matters to bear in mind from the beginning.

The magic 'w's.

Journalists are taught to make sure their stories cover the five 'w's: *Who, what, when, where* and *why*; the crime novels needs to attend to all of these plus an 'h' – *how*.

By the end of your book the reader must, of course, have discovered both who the victim was – and who 'did it'.

They need more though. They need to know what sort of crime has happened, when it happened and where, what one might call the nuts and bolts of the crime. Most importantly, they must discover *why* it happened. What the motivation was for the crime. Even serial killers are motivated to commit their dreadful murders by some aspect of their lives.

Readers also need to know *how* the crime happened. They need the actual details. You may not want to dwell on nasty descriptions of horrifically damaged victims but, as said earlier, there are ways of getting across the facts without making a faint-hearted reader (and the writer) feel they should not have picked up the book. Apart from what actually happened, by the end of the story readers will need to know what led up to the crime, why the victim was chosen and why it was they were in the wrong place at the wrong time.

A successful crime book will reveal all these details bit by bit as the investigation goes forward. The last revelation of all is, of course, the identity of the perpetrator. That is, unless it is one of those books where the reader learns who this is early on. Then the interest of the reader is caught in a different way. Such books can be very effective. Val McDermid's *The Wire in the Blood,* the second of her Tony Hill/Carol Jordan novels, is one such. We know quite quickly who the serial killer is. The reader's attention, instead of wondering about the killer's identity, is held in several other ways. There is the profiling exercise that first links the disappearance and presumed murder of seven teenage girls to the killer, without a shred of evidence to justify a follow-up. Another girl disappears and the trainee-profiling officer who linked together the cluster of disappeared girls is horribly murdered.

The second half of the book is concerned with the attempt by a small band of dedicated officers to tie the killer to the death of his victims. Their efforts are hindered at every stage by the cunning of the killer and official reluctance to accept that the investigation has correctly identified him and so sanction the deployment of large numbers of officers in order to obtain the necessary evidence.

The story is told from several points of view. It includes disturbing descriptions and insights into what can drive the human mind to murder and the part sexuality can play. It is full of suspense and the lack of mystery as to the identity of the murderer is a vital part of a roller-coaster crime novel. The reader is involved in the cat and mouse battle between killer and police and the awful suspense as to whether the killer will strike again before the necessary evidence can be obtained. Finally, it ends on a disturbing note that suggests the battle for justice might not quite be over.

In traditional crime novels, the story works up to a classic denouement during which the investigator reveals the name of the perpetrator, often to an assembled company, amongst whom are several suspects.

Questions are asked on the lines of, 'But I still don't understand why . . . , all of which allows the investigator to uncover the various clues leading to the discovery of the villain, showing exactly who, how and why.

Few successful crime novels lead up to that sort of ending today, unless it is done as parody or an affectionate tip of the hat to the masters, which is what I did at the end of *Appetite for Death*. It is up to the reader to decide the degree of success of this approach.

Today, a crime book will allow the investigation gradually to uncover facts and form theories on the case. The theories will gradually be refined until the evidence, assisted by the sheer intelligence of the protagonist's approach, reveals the perpetrator and allows justice to triumph.

Sounds simple, doesn't it?

The difficulty in bringing a crime novel investigation – whether official or unofficial – to a successful conclusion is managing to end with a bang rather than a whimper. Any 'dying fall', any relaxation of tension, has to come right at the end of the novel, as a sort of coda to the main action. It can come too early if there have to be too many detailed explanations of what has happened, who did what, when and how.

The pace of the story should increase towards the end. It should reach a climax. There should be a final revelation, perhaps a dramatic or violent confrontation.

Keeping true to the book

A book's ending must follow inexorably from what has gone before. This is why endings can reveal themselves to the writer as well as the reader as the story progresses.

Writing a book is a long, hard process. Characters become living beings. We may or may not like all of them (though it is necessary to be able to identify with at least one and care about a few more), but we have accompanied them through life-changing circumstances; we understand them better than many of our dearest friends and relations and we know exactly how they will behave in any situation. To force our characters into an ending that is false merely because it was what we had in mind at the beginning of the book will mean the reader is left unsatisfied. They, too, have got to know the characters, have followed them through all the various twists and turns of the plot, and reacted with them. If the reader cannot believe in the ending, even if it is a happy one, the book will be tossed aside with the reader left with a distinct feeling of being let down and, disastrously, a resolve never to try a book by that author again.

Successful crime novels depend, as does any other novel, on character conflict rather than cerebral puzzles. A crime story has developed the characters that inhabit its pages, changed their lives, altered their relationships, developed them as people. It is not a vehicle for clever clues to the mystery elements that allow the investigator to save up answers until the end of the story.

Denouements

An ending, though, has not only got to be true to what has gone before, it has to be effective.

So much depends on the sort of book you have been writing. A slam-bang thriller climax to a book that has been a cerebral investigation of a crime involving a social problem is unlikely to work. Equally, psychological twists will not wrap up an exciting action-packed novel. Perhaps the best advice to give is that, whatever way you have been writing up to the point where everything comes together and you have your denouement, you have to continue writing in the same way but more intensely. Everything has to become more concentrated.

If your story is action based, the ending has to be more exciting than anything else that has happened so far. Check out Dick Francis. The last stages of his books are always more action-packed than anything that has gone on before and it is almost impossible to put the book down before the last sentence has been read.

If you are writing a traditional mystery where you are keeping the identity of the perpetrator hidden until the end, your reader by then should be desperate for the answer. Events should now follow quickly on one another. You might also find that an action-ending can bring your story to an exciting conclusion – if it can follow naturally out of what has gone before.

It is very important that the author does not cheat, perhaps by suddenly bringing in some completely new development or information. The reader, you hope, will be surprised as all is revealed, but they should not feel dissatisfied. Once they have absorbed the answers to the questions they have been asking, there should be a dawning realisation that, after all, the solution to the mystery had been there all the time. They just failed to see it. Now that readers know what happened, they may go back to the beginning of the book and read it again so they can see what they missed the first time round.

Bringing a psychological mystery to an end offers many possibilities. Again, the intensity has to increase as the complexities of the plot are unravelled. Barbara Vine's *A Fatal Inversion* is a good example; even after the reader assumes they have learned all its secrets, it produces a final twist on the last two pages.

Like *A Fatal Inverson*, the most successful crime books are multi-layered and have asked too many questions for the answers to be brought forth in a single, last, dramatic scene.

If a story is complicated, it has to have a series of resolutions but each one should involve the reader with the outcome of the book a little more deeply. Ian Rankin is a master at bringing a complicated tale to a satisfying finish.

Jessica Mann is one of those to whom the ending is wrapped in mystery, 'Because the story unfolds to me as I write it, I quite often get near the end without being sure myself who has done what to whom, why, and how. Occasionally it takes me months to find the answer and having done so I might go back to the beginning to add clues and change details. So it amuses me that critics often call my books "carefully/neatly/tautly plotted". As for the last line – I know it when I see it, but not till then.'

Successful books often provide the reader with surprises even after the main mysteries have been revealed. Robert Goddard and Harlen Coben are both excellent at producing unexpected twists right at the end. The roots of these twists, though, will have been planted much earlier in the book.

Tie up sub-plots

The various sub-plots you have developed during the course of the book need to be tied up as well as the main plot. You want to make sure that their endings do not interfere with the drama of the main revelations. However, it is sometimes effective to have a sub-plot add a final grace-note to the book, maybe giving the story an upbeat ending. On the other hand, you might use a sub-plot to leave the reader with an unanswered question to avoid too tidy an ending.

Exercise

Take a plot that you have been working on during the reading of this book and decide how you can lead up to a successful ending, then outline the way in which that ending will be written, where it will be set, and what the final surprise to the reader will be.

Writing the ending

Once the ending is clear to you, don't snatch at it.

Like a long distance runner at the end of a marathon, you will be calling on reserves of strength and speed to achieve a successful conclusion to your book. After such a long time, the odds are that you can hardly wait to write THE END. It is a good idea to try to achieve the writing of the last section in one sitting. You should be writing at speed, gripped by the drama of your ending. If you aren't, your reader won't be either. The pace of your story should get quicker and quicker. Your sentences become shorter. Events are thrown at the reader. There is no time to lay groundwork. All that should have been done beforehand.

While you are writing the ending, nothing else should matter but the excitement involved in getting it down. You have spent long hours at the computer or typewriter, now you are at the final stage. The telephone should go unanswered. Someone else walks the dog. The nearest and dearest are told they have to fend for themselves.

A word of warning, though. Many writers, including me, find that writing the last scenes takes longer than expected. Don't be tempted not to give full value to the final denouement – but don't overwrite. The first part of your book is the place for the vivid metaphor and the poetic phrase that can help build atmosphere and illuminate character. At the end of a book, language should be simpler. The reader wants action rather than poetry.

Having written the last part of your book in a white heat, go back and make sure that the reader has been provided not only with action and drama but also all the information necessary to make the ending acceptable. Merely telling the reader which suspect was responsible for the crime is not enough if they can't put together the reasoning that reveals the perpetrator.

The final check

Make sure that you have laid all the necessary groundwork throughout the book. Have you put in place the evidence, the clues, that support your revelations? Laura Wilson says that, as far as clues are concerned, she tries to drop them in as unobtrusively as possible as she writes but, 'quite often I have to go back and re-jig things in order to fit – I've learnt that plotting backwards is just as important as plotting forwards'.

Have you brought all your suspects along the story with you, or have you left one or more in the background after their first entrance? It is no good casting an interesting light on a particular character and making it possible that they are involved in the crime, if the reader then never hears any more about them. Either you need to make sure their part in the events is made clear, or they need to be written out of the plot before you reach the denouement.

What about your villain? Introduced early enough in the book? No reader will be happy to find that the gardener who appears two chapters from the end turns out to be the killer when they have been spending their time wondering about the various suspects introduced in the first few chapters. Quite often the murderer appears early on in the book and then conveniently drops into the background so that they no longer feature in the reader's consciousness. That is fair, as long as that early appearance is enough to impinge properly upon the reader at the time. It is up to the reader to keep all the characters in mind.

It is, though, possible to take the opposite approach and make the murderer such an important character in the book that the reader automatically rejects them as the prime suspect. Remember Agatha Christie's *The Murder of Roger Ackroyd*.

Have you revealed the criminal's motivation to the reader? It may be quite clear to you that it is the murderer's unstable relationship with his prostitute mother that has made him into a serial killer of women with blonde hair who have Poodles, but is the reader as certain?

Has your investigator been in possession of information that hasn't been given to the reader? Or, vice versa, has the reader a vital detail but not the investigator?

Maybe your story has developed in unexpected ways. Do you need to go back and rewrite to foreshadow the developments that weren't in your original scenario?

What about your sub plots? Like the suspects, have you left any characters in a limbo, waiting to know what is to happen to them? Endings need not be too neat but it is unfair to readers to leave them wondering exactly what happened to characters introduced early on but who then faded out of sight. It is also unfair to your reader to develop a promising relationship between a minor character and your protagonist and then leave it hanging. Either promote your minor character into a major one or include a short scene that makes it clear the relationship is not going anywhere. If, though, you are planning a series, you may want the relationship to be unresolved because you intend to develop it in the next book. Then you need to provide a good hint to the reader that that is what is going to happen.

In *Sweet Danger* Margery Allingham introduces her series detective, Albert Campion, to Amanda Fitton, one of the most endearing and idiosyncratic heroines of the golden age of detective fiction. Seventeen years old in *Sweet Danger*, at the end of an exciting denouement in which Amanda is shot and, thanks to her, Campion narrowly escapes death, he visits her sick bed. Amanda says she won't be ready for another six years or so, but, though she isn't proposing marriage, she wants Campion to consider her as a possible partner 'in the business'. The book ends:

> Mr Campion sat where he was for a long time, staring out across the room. His face was expressive, a luxury he scarcely ever permitted himself. At last he rose slowly to his feet and stood looking down very tenderly at this odd little person who had come crashing through one of the most harrowing adventures he had ever known and with unerring instinct had torn open old scars, revived old fires which he had believed extinct.
>
> 'What's going to change you in six years, you rum little grig?' he said slowly.
>
> She did not stir. Her eyes were closed Her lips were parted, and her breath came regularly and evenly.
>
> Amanda was asleep.

The end

Amanda Fitton soon appeared regularly in Margery Allingham's Campion novels.

If you are not sure you want to saddle your protagonist with an ongoing relationship, of whatever sort, better not to raise the possibility. Readers do not like to be disappointed.

When I wrote my first book, I introduced Darina, my protagonist, to a detective sergeant, but flew no flags that the slight friendship, developed during the traumatic events Darina had found herself caught up in, would grow into more. In fact, I didn't know myself that it would. William Pigram just refused to go away and eventually they married.

Jill McGown wrote *A Perfect Match,* a police procedural in which she featured male detective Lloyd and female detective Hill without any intention of making them protagonists in a series. If she had, she may not have made Lloyd a married man. After the book proved to be the first in a series, she eventually sorted matters out so that the two officers could marry.

Exercise

Write the denouement you drafted out earlier in this chapter.

Does it work? Are you, as reader, riveted by what you have written? Have you managed a twist or a coda at the end that will leave the reader not only satisfied but feeling things could not have ended up better? Will they want to read your next book?

Before reaching your denouement you will almost certainly have needed to undertake some research. That is the subject of our next chapter.

Denouements & endings

- ➢ In most crime novels, the villain gets their just desserts and most readers like it that way
- ➢ Endings must cover: who, what, when, where, why and how
- ➢ Endings must be true to what has gone before and in the same spirit
- ➢ Sub–plots must be tied up and fitting fates arranged for most or all characters
- ➢ Endings are best written at white heat and then carefully edited
- ➢ Ensure both reader and investigator are in possession of all the necessary information to solve the mystery
- ➢ Try to give your story a twist or a coda at its very end

11 **Research**

Research is always necessary. However well you know your background and characters, there are always matters that you will need to check.

Alex Gray says, 'a good crime writer will have done his homework to make the background as realistic as possible'. She adds, '... make one wrong move with the details in a crime novel and the whole work comes clattering down like a pack of cards'.

Natasha Cooper advises, 'Don't do too much research before you write. New novelists are endlessly told to write what they know. This can be dangerous because too many facts and explanations act as a drag on the narrative. Once you have a general idea of the background to your novel, write it, noting each place where you need more information. When you've got to the end of the story, find a source of expert knowledge to help you fill in the gaps. This will avoid all those bits of artificial dialogue on the lines of "So, is it true that DNA testing can now establish the physical characteristics of the person who left the saliva/blood/ brain spatters?"'

The value of much of the research you do is not in actually applying it all when writing your book but rather making you feel generally comfortable with what you are writing about. Readers are mostly interested in characters and what happens next. Everything else should be an accessory. Think of it like dressing to go out. Too much jewellery, too flashy clothes, too heavy a fragrance, and those you meet will concentrate on the outfit, fail to see the person wearing it, and pass on to someone they are interested in connecting with.

Location

To start with, you will probably need to research the location of your story. If it is set where you live, you may feel that you know the area well enough. But do you? Practise noticing details every time you go out. Look back at the chapter where we discussed location. It is important to be able to bring the background to your story alive, to know how your characters will react to living there.

If it's set in the country, do the trees slant in a particular way because of the wind? What sort of flowers grow in the hedgerows and exactly how are the hedges kept – are they neatly rounded each autumn or does a machine tear off excess growth leaving whitened ends to the wounded branches? What sort of industrial estate is being built on the edge of your local town? It will be encroaching on the surrounding farmland but has it required a road-widening scheme with a local short-cut closed off for weeks or perhaps months? Is it bringing new jobs into the area?

What is the economy? Expanding with everyone in full employment? Or are there farmers in the depths of depression over the state of agriculture? Has a local industry gone bankrupt throwing people out of work? Are the shops brimming with customers? What is the property situation in the area? Do you take the local paper and know what is happening on the district and county councils? Are there stories which can be used to help add depth to your descriptions?

If you live in a town, can you describe how its architecture has developed over the last hundred years? What is the atmosphere? Is it a dormitory area with a large percentage of inhabitants disappearing every morning to a larger metropolis? Or do the people living in your road work locally? What do they do at the weekends? Where do the young congregate? What goes on in the civic politics? Who are the people regularly featured in the local newspaper? What about property development, is it causing ructions in the community?

Wherever you live, think about the amount and type of crime in the area. Local newspapers are a great source of that and other detail. Make sure you read one at least every few weeks.

When you need to write an outdoor scene, go and visit a similar area, try to find that telling detail that will bring it alive to a reader.

Maybe you aren't setting your story where you live. Go and visit the location you have chosen and research not only its physical features but also its atmosphere, and what sort of people live there, all the points noted above. If you can't make an actual visit, get hold of a good guide to the area, visit the library and try to find a book with illuminating pictures. Sort out examples that capture the unattractive sides of your location as well as the tourist attractions. Get hold of some recent copies of the local paper (the library will have a Press Guide that will tell you which they are and how to contact them).

Michael Jecks says, 'When you write about a place, visit it first. It's not enough to impart a sense of an area by simply imagining it, you have to go there, see the views, experience the weather, study the type of rocks and plants. If you do that right, you can use the landscape as another character. My favourite example of this was Conan Doyle's use of Dartmoor in *Hound of the Baskervilles*, which used the moody, brooding moors to marvellous effect.'

Dreda Say Mitchell's award-winning first novel, *Running Hot*, is set in Hackney and she builds a vivid picture not only of its criminal and ethnic background but also its physical properties, using the comedians Eric Morecombe and Ernie Wise as an analogy:

Aneurin Bevan Tower and Ernest Bevin House stood back to back on the south side of Hackney. The side of Hackney that bumped boundaries with Bethnal Green. In the late 80s the Council had floated the idea of calling them after a couple of Latin American revolutionaries, but tenants and subletters moaned that they had enough trouble trying to wring their tongues around English and Welsh without adding Spanish to the list. So the community had taken charge and unofficially rebaptised both houses Eric and Ernie. Eric was tall and slim, Ernie wide and fat. They should have been a double act, but they weren't. Eric played out the stories of 'I'm giving up tomorrow' junkies, wall scribes and anyone else the Council knew wasn't going to cut it with the rest of the population. High in the sky was the best place for them, some said. Nearer to God's divine grace and as far away as possible from the rest of us. Ernie told a different tale. It dared to be caring, clean, a community.

The story then takes the reader into a flat in Ernie, where the main protagonist of the story lives. The description has added more to our knowledge of him, his background, and the background of the story.

Exercise

An earlier exercise asked you to write a description of a location. Go back and look at it again. Now include some telling detail that will show its basic character.

Historical locations

If you are writing an historical crime novel, go to the local archives in the area you are setting your story, explain what you are doing to the staff and they will be immensely helpful with sources that can build up a picture of your location in the time of your story. Local museums can also yield valuable material. Study maps and descriptions of the period, then go and look at what is there today and try to find the bones of what the place was like in your period. Often there will be buildings of the period. Some will be open to the public and may have their own records. Ilchester is a small Somerset town founded by the Romans. I researched it for a local tourist board leaflet on market towns. In the eighteenth century Town Hall and Community Centre is an ancient map of Ilchester. A study of that made it possible to look at existing features of the town and identify much older periods.

Large towns will have a local reference section in the main library that may yield early guidebooks as well as a good collection of books on the area. I used a library in Bath to research background for *Canaletto and the Case of Bonnie Prince Charlie*. There, amongst much else, I found an excellent description of the turnpike road between London and Bath in the mid-eighteenth century that enabled me to understand how Canaletto and his assistant, Fanny, would have travelled along it. It enabled me to add what I hope were telling details to the account of their journey.

If your historical characters travel between places, find out exactly what sort of transport they could have used and how long it took.

Readers are quick to query the accuracy of research. According to Michael Jecks, 'For me and the Medieval Murderers (a group of crime writers who set their novels in the medieval period), the most common complaint is how far a horse can ride in a day – either we are supposed to travel too far, or not far enough!' There could be genuine discussion on the speed of a horse over unknown territory but there are other matters that should be uncontroversial. Michael Jecks again, 'There is no excuse for getting a date wrong, or not knowing some of the more intricate points of law or the process of justice. If you have a desire to write historical works, you have a duty to be accurate.'

Make the best use you can of libraries. Find the largest in your locality and trawl its shelves for information. Talk to the librarians, they are skilled at knowing where to find what you need.

There is a newspaper library in Colindale, London, and they have an unparalleled collection of newspapers, including microfilm copies of some of the very earliest. The advertisements in these eighteenth century newspapers, together with their editorial stories, illuminate the life of the period with an immediacy that a social history, which will probably have used these very same papers, cannot. It is usually possible to photocopy pages that interest you.

The London Library is a private, subscription library in St James's Square, London W1. It has a vast collection of books; many initially published over two hundred and more years ago. Details of most of the collection are computerised. They have an excellent postal service to supply members with books. One of its aspects that I most value is the fact that you can walk round the stacks and see what books are there, rather than looking up possible volumes in a catalogue (computerised or not) and sending for them while you wait. In some libraries you have to order the day before, if you are not to spend valuable time while the books you want to consult are delivered from some inaccessible repository. Nearly all the London Library books are available for borrowing by members. As with other libraries, the staff are very knowledgeable and most helpful.

Background

Readers love learning about other worlds through a compelling story. A much quoted dictum is to write about what you know. Lindsey Davis says, 'If that were true, I'd be visiting brothels, spearing wild bulls, and using suppositories to seal my will.'

Personal experience, though, can give you confidence and a bank of telling details to draw on. But even if you don't have that authority, it doesn't mean that you can't learn about any sort of background through research, including how to spear wild bulls.

Reading around your subject will give you valuable information but, as previously mentioned, equally important is talking to those who have first hand experience. There is no substitute, in fact, for information from someone who has seen the particular world you are trying to create from the inside. For instance, you might want to set either a part or even a whole book in the sailing world and you've little or no experience of life on the water. Sort out a friend, or a friend of a friend, who sails and find out all you can about the delights and the perils of as many sorts of boats and kinds of sailing as you can. Yacht racing is very different from mucking around in boats. Sailing across the Atlantic, or even the Channel, or round the UK coast, is different again. Even better than talking to someone is to beg, blag or pay your way onto a boat and learn what it is all about at first hand. Look again at the chapter on specialised backgrounds.

Technical questions

With crime books you will always come up against questions involving medicine and forensic science. There are answers to be found, all you have to do is start looking.

Medical detail

When I first started writing crime novels, I rang up a cousin
of my husband's who was a professor of pharmacology
to discuss some plot points connected with poisons. I'd
only met him once or twice at family gatherings, but my
husband assured me he would be very helpful. His first bit
of advice was not to be such an idiot as to know nothing
and he pointed me in the direction of a bookshop at the top
of London's Gower Street, an area thronged with medical
students. I spent a happy time there looking through the
shelves at a vast range of books, both new and used. I finally
bought two used but still highly expensive volumes, one
an encyclopaedia of medicine and one on toxicology. The
investment was well worth it. I have blessed those books
time and again, even though the medical language often
means I have to tease out the information I need, they are
written for professionals in language that the layman at first
sight can find difficult to understand. A medical dictionary
can be helpful when studying such books.

If you don't want to invest in an expensive volume and
have a large hospital nearby, they will have a reference library
you will probably be able to consult.

A great help to me also has been a friend who is a retired GP.
We have had valuable sessions discussing how long poisons
would take to work, the injuries that could be sustained by
someone thrown out of a window, the symptoms for certain
diseases and many other matters.

A writing friend of mine calls in to consult her doctor at
his surgery, timing her visit for the end of his appointment
schedule. She says he is always interested and finds her
questions offer relief from actual patients. He sounds very
sympathetic and is probably unusual. Nevertheless, it is well
worth finding a helpful medic, whether ongoing or retired. If
you put a problem to them, such as the need to find a disease to
match certain symptoms, or the antidotes to certain poisons,
they will almost always be able to supply an answer.

These days the internet is a veritable mine of information
which is available right there at your desk. Try to find sites

that offer expert information and learn to double check facts. Not everything that gets on the web can be trusted. If you don't have internet access at home, your local library will probably offer terminals you can use for free. Do think, though, about acquiring your own. Today's writer really needs a computer and these days almost all offer internet access. Even if you don't want or can't connect to Broadband, there are servers you can sign up to for a very small monthly payment if you are willing to limit your access to certain hours. You will certainly need email when you acquire an agent and a publisher. A great deal these days that used to be conducted by snail mail or fax is now handled electronically.

I value the internet but for me nothing beats wandering along the stacks of a really good library. Researching colonial life in India at the end of the nineteenth century a little time ago at one of my local libraries, I chanced upon a diary of a memsahib written at exactly the time I needed that contained a wealth of interesting detail.

Police procedure

If you are including in your novel, at least in part, a police investigation, you need to be able to create a believable background. I've mentioned already how much can be gained from watching police programmes, both fictional and documentary, on television.

However, never hesitate to ring your local police headquarters and ask to speak to the public relations officer. If you explain that you need background information for a crime novel, they will be most helpful. It is in their interests to make sure you get your facts right. If you can manage to get an introduction to a friendly detective, build a good relationship so that you can go back at another time.

I've been lucky enough to meet a most helpful detective sergeant. My practice is to take him for a quick drink and sandwich at a pub not far from the police station. He seems happy to answer all my questions and usually provides additional information on points that hadn't occurred to me. Once I remember I wanted the detective partner of my cook to go with her to France to check on dental records. What, I wondered, would be the official procedure? My friendly detective wasn't sure, but there was another officer in the pub that day who had only recently come back from undertaking an almost identical operation, and was very happy to fill me in on all the details. That was serendipity but it is amazing how lucky one can be once actively engaged on seeking out information. Who was it who said, 'the harder I work, the luckier I get'?

Remember that each police force works independently. Scotland Yard, now known as the Met (the Metropolitan police force) does not send detectives down to assist local forces in tricky cases. There are critical times, however, when one force can request assistance from another, such as in the December 2006 murder investigation in Suffolk after the discovery, over a very short space of time, of the bodies of several local prostitutes.

There are various police journals, which can be helpful. Joan Lock is a former policewoman who writes both fiction and non-fiction crime and for many years has provided a column on police matters in *Red Herrings,* the monthly journal of the Crime Writers Association (only available to members). She gives the following advice, 'I think *Police Review* is the best bet for budding crime writers. It is the highest circulation police journal published by an independent company rather one with some connection to the police. It was started way back in 1893 by a man who thought the police needed more support. Today it is published by Jane's Information Group. The *Review* covers news, strategy and product developments, comment, police training, letters to the editor, etc. Its coverage is countrywide and illustrates among other things that forces vary a great deal in how they do things. The *Police Review* is weekly. To subscribe, either call the Sub hotline on 01444 475660 or order online from the *Police Review* website, www. policereview.com. If you have crime writing mates, you can pass it around amongst you.'

Joan also says, 'Make friends with your local police, they can be very helpful. Enquire whether the force has a newspaper, which could put you on their mailing list. These vary in helpfulness – some concentrate largely on social matters but at least give you the flavour of the culture. However that of the Metropolitan Police (published online at www.met.police.uk/job/) is professional and has a great deal of good information. A recent issue had features about the Met's Computer Crime Unit, the future of forensics, and people trafficking, referred to as "human cargo". Most police forces now have their own websites which can be very helpful regarding force structure, aims, latest news and the current crimes in their area.'

Finally, Joan suggests reading police biographies/ autobiographies. 'These vary of course – with senior officers you usually discover they were always right!'

Keith Miles advises, 'If you want to write a realistic police procedural, keep abreast of the latest technological aids to policing. Otherwise, you will look out of date. If you set a book in a foreign country, research its law enforcement structure carefully beforehand.'

Again, the internet can produce a great deal of knowledge of use to the writer. Most police procedure has been written down in a series of protocols and they are available on the net. What that sort of information won't give you, however, is the personal angle. How each procedure affects the officer on the case, how they feel about developments, what helps or hinders them doing a good job. For that, you need to talk to actual officers.

You have to remember, too, that fiction cannot always follow reality too closely. Ann Granger says, 'When it comes to police detectives, we all know that police work isn't quite done the way it is in books. An inspector doesn't always work with the same sergeant and he doesn't have just one case on his desk. But a suspension of disbelief is necessary to get a readable story.'

Forensic information

Today much of police evidence is highly technical. A criminal will find it almost impossible not to leave some traces at the scene of the crime and it is up to the Scenes of Crime

Officers to identify what they are. Dorling Kindersley has produced an attractive and instructive book: *Crime Scene,* by Richard Platt (ISBN 0 7513 45768). With the assistance of relevant experts, this book looks at a wide range of the science that lies behind forensic detection. It is lavishly illustrated and contains a considerable amount of easily absorbed information.

If you don't want to get bogged down in forensic detail, or don't trust your ability to deal with the technical aspects, you can avoid much of it by the way you tell your story. You should, though, be aware of the possibilities forensic science can bring to an investigation, how they can trace evidence to a suspect, and how difficult it can be at times for the police to find that suspect and link them to the crime so that DNA, for instance, can be compared. The technology that lies behind forensics is advancing every day and keeping up-to-date can open up possibilities for the successful linking of corpse to killer. For instance, take this snippet from Val McDermid's *The Wire in the Blood*:

> 'Twelve years ago when you killed Barbara Fenwick there were a lot of things forensic science couldn't do. Take toolmarks, for example. Pretty crude, the comparisons they made back then. But these days, they've got scanning electron microscopes and back-scatter electron microscopes. Don't ask me how they work, but they can compare an injury to an implement and say whether the two match up.'

Peter Walker is keen that, 'authors should reflect the advance of technology in their books, particularly in the investigation of crime. Mobile telephones, digital cameras, computers, DNA and advances in forensic science all have their part to play – and, if their work is to be taken seriously, it is the task of writers to carry out the necessary research into these and allied matters.'

One of the things that fascinate me at the moment is the ability of mobile phones to film and send what they film to another telephone or computer. Newspapers and television buy amateur shots from members of the public of disaster scenes, for instance. There is tremendous scope here for the crime novel.

The more you know, the more options will be open to you. If you have some knowledge of the science involved, you will be able to use your expertise in many different ways and increase the impact of your story.

As I've said before, never be afraid of approaching specialists. Most people love talking about what they do.

Pictures

Never neglect pictures as a reference source. Photographs are an invaluable help. Wherever you go, take snaps of places, buildings, people, particularly of places you may not visit again, and always identify exactly where and when they have been taken as soon as you have a print (would that I had taken my own advice!). Even if your location is imaginary, pictures of a similar place can help with the writing.

If you are writing a book set in the past, you need references for clothes, home life, street life, every kind of life, and there are very useful published collections of period photographs, often from news magazines such as *Picture Post*. They cover a wide range of everyday subjects, as well as great occasions and those that hit the headlines. Scan them with careful eyes. Sometimes a photograph of a celebrity could be passed over as irrelevant but look at the background before you reject it entirely. Often there is detail there that can be of use.

For the eras before photography, paintings are a wonderful source of information on dress, jewellery, interior decoration and many other details. Remember that usually such paintings capture their subjects looking their best and making the most of their background. But not all show aristocrats or society life, there are glimpses of industry, humble backgrounds, sporting occasions, and such subjects as railway termini.

Television is a rich source of information, particularly for crime stories. Quite apart from the programmes featuring the police mentioned earlier, there are programmes on many aspects of crime, some of which have interviews with ex-criminals. Look out for programmes on areas you are interested in: backgrounds, travel pieces, memoirs. There are many programmes that could be of help, all of them contain film and still photography to illustrate their subject. Always be ready to record anything that will be useful.

Television can be brilliant at capturing characters, not only those in the news, but ordinary or not-so-ordinary people talking about some aspect of their lives. Tricks of speech, the way they look, their expressions as they talk about matters that move, amuse or embarrass them; all can be valuable to a writer. If you use video tapes or CD discs to record programmes, keep them, clearly marked, on a special shelf or in a box so that they are easy to find when you need to refer to them again – and so that no one records over them!

Exercise

Take one of the characters you have created at some stage of working through this book, assess how much information you will need in order to make them come to life and to be able to describe their world, then make a plan of how you would research the necessary details.

Indentifying research

Whatever sort of research you do, keep accurate notes that identify the source.

Acquire a cassette recorder and a supply of tapes. Always ask an interviewee if they mind being recorded. If they refuse permission, take as many notes as you can manage during the interview then write it up immediately afterwards. As you transcribe your notes, what you've written down will remind you of a great deal more of what they told you, especially those little details that you can never find in books. If they are happy for you to record them, mark the tape with the name of the interviewee and the date you recorded them. Again, keep the tapes somewhere handy.

If you cut or tear out articles, photographs, news stories from papers or magazines, write on them where it's come from and the date it was printed.

When making notes from books, the name, author and publisher of the book and page number/s should form part of your notes. You may well have to recheck a fact.

Verification

When you have written your book, try to get an expert to read through the bits that refer to specialist knowledge. It is very easy to get the atmosphere or an emphasis wrong, or even get facts wrong. Your book may be fiction but an inaccurate detail can destroy the authority of your story. If a reader finds the author has made an error, whatever it is, they may start to wonder what else in the book is incorrect and the story will fail to hold them.

At last you have written your book. What do you do now? In the last chapter we will deal with preparing your book for submission and how to find a publisher.

Research

> Research everything you need to make your story authentic
> Make certain your facts are accurate
> Use libraries, the internet, television, radio, interviews with experts, photographs, paintings.
> Keep cuttings from magazines and newspapers
> Take photographs of locations, etc, with details of when and where
> Write up interviews with specialists as soon as possible
> Try to get the specialist parts of your work checked by experts

12 Selling Your Book

Your book is finished. Hooray! Treat yourself to a drink and a good meal. Then get down to selling it.

First, you need to make sure your book is as good as you can make it. You also need to ensure that it is in a format that agents and publishers will find acceptable.

Length

In the Golden Age of crime fiction, the length of a book by such authors as Agatha Christie and Margery Allingham was around 60,000 words, roughly the same amount as this book. Gradually, over the years, length has crept up. My crime novels, and those of many others, are around 90,000. But there are more and more books that are longer. If your book is over 100,000 words, make sure that the story can sustain that length. Is the plot over-complicated? Are there too many characters? Is there any sort of repetition? Is your writing too leisurely? Could you use a blue pencil with advantage? Usually removing everything that isn't absolutely necessary to your story will improve it. Phrases, such as 'he said regretfully', 'she said belligerently', should usually go. Very often you can say something more effectively with fewer words. Remember Andrew Taylor's maxim, '*Less is more*'.

A good test as to whether anything can or should be cut is to ask: will it harm the story if I take it out? If something isn't necessary to some aspect of your book, if it isn't vital to the plot, doesn't illuminates character, isn't a clue or a red herring, or doesn't create the right setting or atmosphere for a scene, then cut. Even if it means removing a passage you believe is one of the best things you've ever written. Some would say, especially if you think it is one of the best things you've ever written! Very often such gems are self-indulgent.

Title

Does your book have a good title? Did you start writing it knowing what it was going to be called or are you still wondering?

Titles can come in a flash or may have to be agonised over. There are authors who scan the *Oxford Book of Quotations* trying to find something apt. Sometimes the perfect quote has already been used. How many authors have cursed Hemingway for lighting on *Ode to a Nightingale* and pinching *Tender is the Night*? Ruth Dudley Edwards chose *Murder in the Cathedral* for her crime novel satirising the Church of England. This is also the title of T S Eliot's well-known play about Thomas à Becket and Henry II, but there is not much likelihood of any confusion between the two. There is, in fact, no copyright in titles and there are examples of more than one novel being published under the same one, but the last thing you want is someone muddling up your book with another. You could flash your choice up on Amazon.com and see if anything comes up, or ask your friendly local bookseller to try it on his computer. If it doesn't appear, you are probably safe.

It is a useful exercise to scan the titles of new crime novels in a large bookshop. This could give a feel for the sort of title that authors and publishers are currently going for since, as in everything else, there tends to be a fashion in titles. Something short and crisp, however, is almost always popular. It is best to choose one that gives a flavour of the book. I wrote a whole series of books with titles that contained the word 'Death'. My intention was to link the books as a series and to indicate that they were connected with crime. However, I think the time for that sort of reference has passed. The book I'm working on now, which may or may not turn out to be the first of a series, will have a very different sort of title. My historical mysteries featuring Canaletto all start: *The Case of. . .*, which was an eighteenth century nod to the *Perry Mason* series but which would also, I hoped, firmly identify the books as mysteries.

Peter Lovesey once did an exercise jotting down the ten most memorable crime novel titles he could think of and found that they all began with 'The'. Also that they raised some sort of question in the reader's mind: *The Spy Who Came in From the Cold,* was one of his choices, another was *The Thirty-nine Steps.* Then there was *The Day of the Jackal.* They are all titles, said Peter, which are intriguing and would make us pick up the book if we saw it in a bookshop. If we can make a potential reader pick up ours, we could be on our way. Peter's first book was *Wobble to Death.* It may not start with 'the' but it is immediately intriguing. It is also a clever introduction to a nineteenth century crime story set around cycle racing.

Peter leaves finding a title as a treat in store for when he's finished a book. 'I work out a top ten and then eliminate until there are three left. Then, out nowhere, it seems, comes the only possible title, utterly different from the ones I've been playing with. Only rarely have I thought of the title while writing the book.' Peter's titles always mean the book is picked up: *The Detective Wore Silk Drawers, Bertie and the Crime of Passion,* and *Bloodhounds,* are just three of them.

One-word titles have impact. Michael Dibdin's *Ratking,* set in Italy, fulfilled the title's promise by winning the CWA Gold Dagger for best crime novel of the year. I've already mentioned Denise Mina's *Garnethill,* another award-winning book. Two word titles can be equally effective. Dick Francis has hardly ever used more than two words and his titles always contain clever allusions and plays on words: the four novels involving his only series character, the one-handed ex-jockey Sid Halley, illustrate this perfectly: *Whiphand, Odds Against, Come to Grief,* and, the now well-known, *Under Orders.*

There are titles that send a shiver down the spine: John Baker's *Walking With Ghosts* and Margaret Murphy's *Caging the Tiger* come to mind. They are infused with suspense and danger.

P D James has chosen from a range of approaches for her titles. She has had long ones: *An Unsuitable Job for a Woman* and *The Skull Beneath the Skin,* for instance. She beat me to the draw with a title I had in mind for one of my novels: *A Taste for Death* (I adapted mine to *A Tasty Way to Die*). Much shorter was *Devices and Desires,* a title that reverberates in the mind, and, another intriguing one, *Original Sin.*

Ruth Rendell is another master crime writer who has a way with intriguing titles. From her considerable output, here are just a few: *From Doon With Death* (her first novel), *The Best Man to Die, Shake Hands Forever, Kissing the Gunner's Daughter,* all novels featuring her series detective, Wexford. Then there's *Vanity Dies Hard, A Demon in My View* (which won the CWA Gold Dagger), *The Keys to the Street.* Writing as Barbara Vine, her titles include: *A Dark Adapted Eye, A Fatal Inversion* (another CWA Gold Dagger winner), and *Gallowglass.*

Final manuscript checks

If you haven't already done so, print out your manuscript. A typescript reads differently from a work on-screen. I don't know why this should be so, but it is. You may well find that you need to make alterations as you read the typescript and you will almost certainly find typing errors. A computer check with word-spell will point up a lot of errors but it will not mark up words that are wrong but still acceptable words. For instance if you type 'there' for 'their', or 'it's' where it should be 'its' (and believe me it is easy to do this) or leave the end 'd' off 'agonised', the computer will assume that the words are correct. Another trap is that your own eye will often see what it expects rather than what is there. A good idea is to find a friend who will read your manuscript and mark any errors, including those involving punctuation marks (it is easy to include an unnecessary comma, or to omit one that is necessary, or a quotation mark or full stop). Make sure the friend is someone whose opinion you respect as they will probably give you feed-back on the story itself. Such feed-back could involve a certain amount of rewriting but may mean a better book in the end. On the other hand, it is your book and friends can be wrong!

Take the time to read your final work out loud. I've already mentioned this but it bears repetition. There is no better way to discover if your prose will carry the reader along without hesitation.

Perform a continuity check: are the eyes that are blue on page two still blue on page two-hundred and two? Do all your characters have the same name all the way through? This is not as daft as it may sound. I regret to have to admit that I wrote a book with a character called by one name on his first appearance who then disappeared for a sizeable number of chapters. By the time he reappeared towards the end of the book, he had acquired a different name. I didn't pick it up and nor did either of the editors who worked on the book. It took an alert reader to write in and point it out just in time to make the necessary corrections before the book went into paperback.

Advice from Michael Jecks, 'If there is bad grammar or spelling or repetitive use of the same word in the first two pages, the editor won't go further. Shoddiness is a turn-off for people who enjoy concision and precision.'

Format

All the usual rules apply for the final printing of your manuscript: use one side of the page only with one-and-a-half line or double spacing (I have to bless Peter Lovesey for pointing out that he found one-and-a-half line spacing, which takes up less paper, acceptable to publishers). If you don't have a computer, be aware that any typed submission these days is treated with suspicion. It suggests a writer who hasn't kept up with modern technology and could be difficult to communicate with in this age of email.

If you are printing via a computer, do not go for fancy type-faces, they will not be appreciated. Straight-forward Times New Roman or Courier are very acceptable and probably the safest choice you can make.

Prepare a covering sheet with the title of the book centred in the middle of the page, with the author's name you want to use (it might be a pseudonym) under that. In the bottom left hand corner say who the copyright belongs to: i.e.: Copyright: Your name (not a pseudonym). Add your address, telephone and email details. On the right hand side state the length of the book, rounding up or down to the nearest thousand words.

The first page of the ms should state the title of the book, the 'by' line, and then Chapter One, plus the chapter title if you are using these (which is up to you, many authors merely number chapters). Each line should be centred:

Death Came At Midnight
by
J D Nobody

CHAPTER ONE
The Chimes Sound

The first paragraph of each chapter and after any break in the text should start at the left hand margin. Subsequent paragraphs should be indented. Do not justify the script. I know that in books the print is justified, that is, lined up on both margins of the page, but editors do not like to see this in an ms. Only the left hand margin should be straight. This is the accepted way of setting out an ms, you may have other ideas but if you want your book to stand the best chance of being read with an open mind, follow tradition – at least until you are a best seller. Use margins of at least two and a half centimetres.

Once you are quite happy that there is nothing you wish to correct or change in your book, it is time to press the button for the final print out. By all means have it ready for email and on a floppy disc to be snail-mailed if either should be required but agents and publishers still prefer to receive a manuscript, especially one that is unsolicited, in hard copy – in other words a typescript.

Don't fasten the pages in any way but place them in a wallet file or, if you are sending too many pages for one of these, a box of the sort used for A4 writing paper.

You will not need to send the whole of your book to the agent or publisher you hope will take you on. Usually the first three chapters are submitted or, if they are very short, ensure you have sent around 3,000 to 5,000 words. Prepare another version of the cover page where you state on the bottom right hand side a line such as: First 5000 words submitted of 95,000 word novel (or whatever length your book is). Remainder available on application.

Selling your book

Selling your book is as difficult, sometimes more so, than actually writing it.

Equip yourself with a copy of one of the two annual Writer's handbooks: *The Writer's and Artist's Guide* published by A & C Black, *The Writer's Handbook* by Macmillan. You should find them in the reference section of a decent library but it is well worth buying one for yourself. Both of the books list up-to-date information on publishers and agents and a great deal else besides. Unless you are extremely lucky, the sections on publishers and agents will soon be well-thumbed.

Basic guidelines

The entry given for each publisher and agent in the writer's guidebooks will identify whether they could be interested in crime fiction. Make two lists of names, one for publishers and one for agents.

A visit to a bookshop and a talk with the member of staff dealing in crime fiction could help identify which publishers are likely to be interested in the sort of book you have written. Make a list of their names. These should be the first you approach. However, there are more and more small presses in existence these days and bookshops may not be acquainted with all of them. The Maia Press, who published the award-winning *Running Hot,* has an entry in the 2007 Writer's Handbook stating that they only produce six titles a year.

Few publishers these days will look at an unsolicited ms. On occasion, the handbook will register this fact. If it doesn't, a phone call could ascertain if a particular publisher will consider the first 3,000 – 5,000 words of your book, together with a short synopsis of the remainder.

But you may do better if you can acquire an agent rather than looking for a publisher. Authors sometimes balk at giving away ten per cent or more of their earnings. That commission should be worth paying. In the first place, agents ought to be able to negotiate better terms for writers than they can themselves. More importantly, though, agents should know which publisher is best for which work and can maximise returns by way of subsidiary rights, foreign rights and pursuing publishers for laggard payments. In fact an author with a half-way reasonable agent should be receiving a great deal more after the agent has taken their cut than they would earn on their own.

More and more agents today edit clients' work before it reaches the publisher, important now that fewer and fewer editors can afford to spend much time on this themselves. Publishers seem to require a book they buy to be ready for publication without additional work; one of the many reasons why they often won't consider a manuscript unless it's presented through an agent.

Entries for agents in the writer's handbooks will give details of how to apply to be added to their list of authors. Often initial contact is limited to a covering letter, a curriculum vitae and a synopsis of your book. Call and check the name of the person you should write to. Sometimes names are included in the handbooks but it's always best to check that there hasn't been a change. Some agents charge a reading fee but should then give you a critique of some sort. If you ring them before sending in your work, you could ascertain what you can expect in return for your fee.

Make sure you send what is asked for. If it's only a CV and synopsis, do not assume that they will read your book if you send the ms anyway. Always include an SAE. You may not want your details or first few chapters back but the publisher or agent will not wish to incur postage costs even if all they want to do is acknowledge and say *'thanks but no thanks'*.

Points to get over

Before approaching either an agent or a publisher, spend time getting together a good presentation of yourself and your work. Remember, though, that it's the content, not the packaging that's important. Write a short CV and include anything you have done that could be turned into publicity. Publishers will need promotional material when they issue your first book and if the background or theme of the book can be tied to your experiences, so much the better. You may, for instance, have appeared on the television programme *Big Brother,* or one of the multitude of other reality shows. Perhaps you may have set up a refuge home for injured birds, or orphans in India. If you have newsworthy relations, include details.

The covering letter to your submission, whether it is merely a synopsis or the first few chapters, should be short. Always remember that you are contacting extremely busy people and that the quicker you can get their attention the better. But a good covering letter could interest the recipient in the rest of your submission. If it's sloppily written, the ms won't stand a chance of being read.

In your letter make clear if you intend writing a series, which is what many publishers of crime fiction look for.

Mention any particular expertise you have made use of in your book. When I sent in the first of my culinary mysteries, I said that I was a food writer, with the implication that I knew what I was writing about. I also said that I planned a series of books, each of which would look at a different area of the food world.

Any publishing experience at all, articles in the local newspaper, for instance, short stories, etc, should be mentioned. They will give added authority to your writing and prove that you know about using words.

There are magazines published for writers that run competitions for short stories, poetry and other types of writing. Entering these may provide you with published work and will certainly accustom you to meeting deadlines.

So, to sum up, you need to work on:

a) your covering letter
b) a synopsis and
c) a curriculum vitae.

Here's what each should contain:

Covering letter

A covering letter is the first thing of yours a prospective publisher or agent will see; it needs to make the right impression and to get over the following information:

> Who you are
> The title and a two-line description of your book
> The fact that you are sending a short synopsis and (if you are) the first part of the book
> State whether your book is finished (much the best) or the date on which it will be finished
> Whether you intend the book to be the first of a series (often liked by publishers of crime novels)
> The fact that you are a published writer (if you are)

Make your letter short, no more than a page. Always remember that you are contacting extremely busy people and that the quicker you can get their attention the better.

Synopsis

A really good synopsis can be a great help in selling a book. It should:

> Give the title and word length of your book
> Be written in the present tense and in the third person
> Give a summary of the story that will include character, conflicts, motivation
> Not include dialogue
> Avoid repetition, redundancies, unnecessary adjectives and adverbs

> Reflect a flavour of the book
> Be as short as possible, preferably one to three pages

It is a lot to ask for and will almost certainly take several drafts to get right. Study the 'blurbs' on books for lessons on how to get over plot lines simply, but avoid any sensationalism or over-writing. Remember a synopsis is a sales tool. You want to convince anyone who looks at it they have to read your book. It should demonstrate that you are a professional who can tell a good story and have the technical skills needed to produce the finished work.

Curriculum vitae

This should get over what your experience is and why you could be of interest. Remember that you are not applying for a job, you are selling a book. Concentrate on:

> Writing experience, i.e.: brief details of published work – articles, poetry, short stories, books – any copywriting you may have done, anything that demonstrates you know about words and deadlines
> 'Award winning' should be stated if relevant, whatever the award was for – you don't have to give details
> Details of any background relevant to your work
> Any details that could help promote you and your book
> Names of any famous relations

It is always worth ringing an agent before sending in a submission, it can save you postage and paper. Some agencies may have enough authors on their books and do not wish to consider taking on any more. There is a limit to the number that can be handled effectively and an effective agent is what you are looking for.

If you ring, you may be asked what sort of book you have written. Make sure you have ready a short description of your book. 'Short' means just that. You need to make a pitch of no more than a sentence or two. For instance: A twin murders and takes the place of her sister who has just married a famous TV wild-life presenter. A photographer friend of the murdered twin suspects the substitution but would have to admit to a crime if she makes an accusation so chooses to investigate instead; an investigation that leads to a dramatic denouement in the Gobi desert.

If the company you send your synopsis or first few chapters to requests the remainder of your manuscript, sing a little song and send it off immediately. A lapse of time could mean they lose interest and focus on some other writer.

Remember that an agent and a publisher both look for an author whose work is saleable and will be able to keep writing more books that they can handle.

Make sure that whatever you send is well set out and absolutely pristine. No corrections, no fingerprints, no smudges or coffee stains; nothing to suggest it has been hanging around or sent to anyone else previously.

Exercise

Produce a synopsis of your novel in three pages or less. Then prepare a 'blurb', a description that would be suitable for a jacket cover. Finally, create a 'pitch' for it in no more than two sentences.

The Crime Writers' Association Debut Dagger

The Crime Writers' Association runs an annual competition for new writing. It was first run in 1998 and since then every winner has been taken up by a publisher, plus many of the runners-up. Joolz Denby was the first winner with *Stone Baby*. Several books later she was short-listed for the Orange Prize for Fiction. Barbara Cleverly, a runner-up in 1999 won the 2004 CWA Ellis Peters Historical Dagger. The competition organiser in 2005 was Edwin Thomas. A runner-up in 2001, he signed two substantial publishing deals and now writes full time.

The Debut Dagger asks for the opening 3000 words of a potential crime novel, together with a short synopsis of the story. The competition is open to anyone writing in English, including those from overseas, who has not yet had a novel commercially published. The CWA takes a broad view of what constitutes a crime novel: previous winning entries have ranged from the mean streets of Los Angeles to the bloody human sacrifices of Aztec Mexico; from the lonely perils of the Australian outback to a serial killer in Bradfield.

Entry at the time of writing costs £10 with a first prize of £250 plus a night in a London hotel for two. All short-listed entrants receive an invitation to the CWA Awards ceremony, where they have a chance to meet leading crime writers, editors and agents.

Visit the CWA web site: www.thecwa.co.uk for up-to-date information on how to enter.

Other options

If you fail to find an agent or a publisher, take a look at internet and self-publishing options.

The internet is such a volatile area; it is difficult to keep up with publishing opportunities. So far few openings seem likely to offer much in the way of financial returns but the exposure might be worthwhile. Check the Writers' Handbooks already mentioned to see if they can offer advice. Check the web itself.

Self-publishing can sometimes sound tempting. But be careful not to get enmeshed in what is known as vanity publishing. You may have seen advertisements for companies seeking to publish books; this is usually provided the author underwrites the production costs. Most of these companies are in the business of taking an author's money and not in selling books; costs can run into several thousand pounds. Very rarely is much in the way of editing provided or much effort made to sell the book. Often not all the print run is bound, only enough for the author to provide copies for friends and relations. More cost is then involved if the writer wants to try to sell it to bookshops themselves. Vanity publishing should be avoided at all costs.

There are some publishing houses that pick and choose authors and ask for a contribution to costs rather than the whole amount. Investigate any such very carefully before agreeing to hand over any money. A local bookshop might be able to offer advice.

'Self-publishing' means you organise the production and printing of your book yourself, which should involve much less money than vanity publishing. Quotations from at least three different printers are recommended. If you can have your book professionally edited and designed, so much the better. Alison Baverstock's book, *Marketing Your Book, An Author's Guide,* published by A & C Black, ISBN 0-7136-5965-3 contains invaluable advice on this and other aspects of getting your book published and marketed. Alison is currently preparing a second edition of her book. She says, 'Since 2001 (when the book was first published), a number of key things have changed within the book business, most notably the cheapness with which authors can have their own website; the vastly increased number of people writing; the huge rise in literary festivals and reading circles.' The new edition promises to be even more useful than the original.

The key to self-publishing is being able to sell your books. Of course you believe your crime novel will be a riveting read for a wide variety of people but can you make them aware of its existence? Advertising can be highly expensive and bring little return. Keeping large quantities of books in good condition requires a damp-proof storage area (few garages qualify). Packing and sending out books is time-consuming and expensive. So is trying to sell-in to bookshops. However, various authors have managed it and today's printing technology means that it is possible to produce books on-demand, which could simplify the whole operation.

Keep writing

All the time you are contacting publishers and agents, keep writing! Ruth Rendell once said that the moment she has finished one book, she starts the next.

If a publisher knows the follow-up book is already written, it could prove attractive, and may help to sell the first. Or the second book may be the one that finds an agent or sells to a publisher.

I find that as I get towards the end of one book, so ideas for the next start coming. I need time, though, to plan before writing what for me are magic words: CHAPTER ONE. Even after considerable preparation and planning, I usually stall after writing these magic words and wonder exactly how to start. When I do put down the first sentences, more often than not, I think again and rewrite. But the process has started.

Writing doesn't always pour out. There are wonderful times when you seem merely a typist taking dictation; your mind is producing words without you thinking about them. You read them back and wonder where they came from! Other times you find yourself having to stop and think all the time. You go back and rewrite. You alter the story line, rethink motivation, adjust the story and where it is going. Finally, though, the writing is once more flowing.

There is a condition known as 'writer's block', where it seems impossible to move ahead with your writing. Not everyone believes in it. Michael Jecks says, 'If you ever think you have writer's block, ask yourself whether you really want to be a writer. A writer will write, no matter what. It could be, as authors often say, that what you write is complete twaddle or crap. No matter. Rubbish can always be thrown away. But no professional writer of my acquaintance suffers from block. Only those with hugely inflated bank balances can afford this affectation. If you are a writer, a serious, professional writer, you have a job to do. Get on with it!'

Ruth Dudley Edwards agrees, 'There is no such thing as writer's block. Just sit down and get on with it. When a problem seems intractable, go and do something else and leave it to your subconscious, your best friend.'

Peter Lovesey seldom suffers from writer's block. 'I certainly have times when I find it very hard to move, but I edge round the obstruction simply persevering until the breakthrough comes. It always does, the flow returns and I'm away again. The planning helps here because I know where the book is going.'

I can't say I have ever had the sort of writer's block that prevents one from writing for weeks, months, sometimes years. But there have been occasions when I can't seem to move forward with my current book. I then try to identify why. Is the plot in trouble? Have I not got deeply enough inside the character I'm dealing with at this point? Am I labouring over something that needs to be neatly skimmed over so I can get to the next interesting scene?

Sometimes the difficulty has been with something outside my writing. Working on a book very often blanks out the personal world but not always. Once I recognise this, I usually manage to do something about the problem. It doesn't always go away but the fact I know about it seems to unlock the creative juices.

Ruth's advice to go away and do something else often works.

If everything else fails, I start to retype the last six or seven pages of the book, copying what I have already done. Soon I start altering what is there and not long after that, I find I'm back in the swing.

One of the greatest aids to keeping going is working at your book every day. Have a target, either a certain number of words or an amount of time. Make sure you set it at a low level. That way you avoid failure and feel good when you achieve much more than your target. Writing every day means that you keep the story in your mind. Even when you aren't actually writing, your subconscious keeps working on it. When you go to bed, go over in your mind what you want to write tomorrow – in the morning, you should find you are ready to go. Try not to finish your daily stint at an awkward stage, make it easy to start writing the next day.

Never, ever, throw away stuff you have written. A scene you have discarded as not working in your current book may, with a little rewriting, fit happily into another one. You may not want to finish a book you have been working on for any one of a number of reasons but don't put it in the dustbin. Shove it in a drawer. Later, perhaps after writing one or more other books, you may be able to see it in a whole new light. If you never find any use for discarded material, it doesn't matter, but it's often easier to rework a passage than to create one from scratch.

Keep writing, keep reading, keep plotting. And good luck!

Selling your book

- ➤ Make sure your manuscript is as perfect as possible
- ➤ Research publishers and/or agents who could be interested in your book
- ➤ Ring possibilities before sending off anything
- ➤ Have ready a very, very short description of your book
- ➤ Be prepared to send the first 3,000-5,000 words of your book with a synopsis of the rest
- ➤ Keep your synopsis short and to the point
- ➤ Write a good covering letter
- ➤ Send a short CV
- ➤ Print your manuscript in 1-1/2 or double line spacing, unjustified on the right hand side
- ➤ Have a cover page giving title, author's name, copyright ownership, contact details and length of book
- ➤ Consider entering for the CWA Debut Dagger
- ➤ Start on your next book as soon as have finished your first

THE END

Appendix I

Useful Books

Make sure your shelves have an authoritative dictionary, a thesaurus, a dictionary of names, one of quotations, and a good book on grammar – the Oxford University Press produces good examples of them all. You will find other reference books necessary as you continue writing.

One or other of the following guides is essential, new editions are published each year:

Writers' & Artists' Yearbook, A & C Black

The Writer's Handbook, Macmillan

Creative Advice:

There are any number of books with useful advice and information for creative writers. Those I think are particularly useful for the crime writer (not all are still in print but are still worth tracking down) are:

Writing Crime Fiction, H R F Keating, A & C Black, 1994

Bloody Murder – From the Detective Story to the Crime Novel: a History, Julian Symons, Faber & Faber 1972

Writing Crime & Suspense Fiction and getting published, Lesley Grant-Adamson, Hodder & Stoughton 1996

Writing Mysteries, Second Edition, edited Sue Grafton, Second Edition by the Mystery Writers of America, Writer's Digest

Two 'how to' books written by crime writers:

Writing the Novel, Lawrence Block, Writers' Digest Books, Cincinnati, Ohio, 1979

Write Away, Elizabeth George, Hodder & Stoughton, 2004

A writer who is more suspense than crime but is essential reading:

On Writing, Stephen King, Hodder & Stoughton, 2000

Books by agents (they know the market):

From Pitch to Publication, Carole Blake, Pan Macmillan 1999

Writing the Breakout Novel, Donald Mass, Writer's Digest 2001

Technical detail:

For up-to-date information on any aspect, search Amazon.com, but check all facts.

Two basic books that give good background detail and include true crime detail:

Crime Scene – the ultimate guide to forensic science, Editor Richard Platt, Dorling Kindersley 2003

Crime Scene Investigation, Introduction Cyril H Wecht, MD, JD, Reader's Digest, 2004

Two other books that contain fascinating information:

A Suitable Job for a Woman: Inside the World of Women Private Eyes, Val McDermid, Poisoned Pen Press 1995

Urge to Kill, Martin Edwards, Writer's Digest

Appendix II

I am immensely grateful to the following crime writers who so generously responded to my appeal for crime writing advice. Only the briefest of details of their books is given. Apply to their websites for further information, and seek out their work in bookshops:

Natasha Cooper

Natasha has written two crime series, one featuring the 'tongue-in-cheek' Willow King, the other barrister Trish Maguire. As Clare Layton, Natasha has also begun writing a new series looking at the effects of crime rather than the investigation.

Judith Cutler

Two crime series, one with amateur sleuth, Sophie Rivers, the other featuring Detective Sergeant Kate Power, both set in Birmingham.

Lindsey Davis

A long series of award-winning crime novels featuring *Falco*, a Roman 'informer', which cover a wide variety of historically accurate settings.

Ruth Dudley Edwards

A series of satirical crime novels set in the world of the Establishment. Ruth is also a main stream non-fiction writer

Martin Edwards

Crime series featuring Liverpool lawyer Harry Devlin, a psychological suspense novel *Take My Breath Away*, and eight non-fiction books including an account of homicide investigation, *Urge to Kill*. Published by Writer's Digest.

Liz Evans

Crime series set on England's South Coast featuring spirited Private Investigator Grace Smith.

Robert Goddard

Over fifteen best-selling complex mysteries that keep the reader guessing.

Paula Gosling

An American by birth but living in the UK since the 1960s, many of Paula Gosling's books are set in the US. Three crime series and a number of stand alone crime novels, winner of several awards. Has recently started writing historical crime.

Ann Granger

Two modern crime series: the 'Meredith & Markby' books pairing a female foreign service officer with a policeman are set in a Cotswold village; the Fran Varaday series with a young, amateur sleuth in London. Ann Granger has now started writing historical crime novels.

Alex Gray

Crime series set in Glasgow featuring Chief Inspector Lorimer.

Reginald Hill

Two crime series, one of over twenty award-winning books featuring Andy Dalziel and Peter Pascoe of Mid-Yorkshire CID which has successfully transferred to television, the other starring the ex-lathe operator turned Private Investigator Joe Sixsmith. Reginald Hill has also written thrillers under the pseudonym Patrick Ruell, and books in a number of other genres. Amongst other awards, he has received the Cartier Diamond Dagger for a lifetime contribution to crime writing.

Russell James

Some ten noir stand-alone crime novels that investigate various aspects of the UK underworld.

Michael Jecks

Over twenty historical crime novels set in medieval-times West Country featuring Bailiff Simon Puttock and local squire space Sir Baldwin.

Peter Lovesey

Over twenty crime novels, including three series featuring Victorian police sergeant Cribb; Bertie, Prince of Wales; and the contemporary detective, Chief Inspector Diamond, set in Bath. Recipient of many awards, Peter Lovesey has also been awarded the CWA Gold and Silver Daggers and the Cartier Diamond Dagger.

Val McDermid

More than twenty crime novels include three series featuring: the lesbian Lindsey Gordon; the PI Kate Brannigan; and the psychological profiler Tony Hill and police detective Carol Jordan, now the basis of the successful TV series, *Wire in the Blood*. Her many awards include the CWA Macallan Gold Dagger.

John Malcolm

Fourteen crime novels featuring Tim Simpson, art investment adviser.

Jessica Mann

Over twenty novels of mystery and suspense, six of which feature the archaeologist Tamara Hoyland.

Keith Miles

Over forty novels, some of them for children. As Edward Marston, has published a number of historical crime series, the most recent set in the world of the nineteenth century railway. Other pseudonyms are Martin Inigo and, in the US, Conrad Allen. As Keith Miles has written a number of contemporary murder mysteries set in the golf world.

Susan Moody

Author of two series of crime novels, one featuring six fool tall, rich and black Penny Wanawake, the other bridge-playing Cassandra Swann, plus a number of suspense thrillers. She has also written romantic novels, three as Susan Madison, and edited The Hatchards Crime Companion.

Ian Rankin

Seventeen novels in the acclaimed Inspector Rebus series, adapted into a major TV series, three thrillers writing as Jack Harvey, and an early spy novel.

Zoe Sharp

Five books in series featuring sparky Charlie Fox, self-defence instructor.

Andrew Taylor

Around sixty books, mainly crime novels and thrillers, including the Roth Trilogy; the Lydmouth series of fifties' detective novels; the Dougal series featuring an eccentric detective who occasionally commits murder himself. Amongst many awards are the John Creasey Dagger for best crime debut novel, and the CWA Ellis Peters Historical Award, the only writer so far to win it twice.

Peter N Walker

Over one hundred books (some on Yorkshire), most written as Nicholas Rhea, including the Constable series, basis for the popular *Heartbeat* TV series. Other major series feature: Detective Inspector Montague Pluke, a man with a passion for horse troughs; and Detective Superintendent Mark Pemberton. Peter Walker started publishing under his own name with the Carnaby series and all his novels reflect his experiences in the police and his beloved Yorkshire countryside.

Laura Wilson

Nine psychological crime novels.

Acknowledgements

The excerpts from published texts included in *Writing Crime – Making Crime Pay* have been quoted by kind permission of the following (note that unless otherwise stated copyright resides with the author):

Marjorie Allingham, *Tiger in the Smoke* (p9 Penguin edition 1957). Copyright: 1952 Rights Limited, a Chorion company. All rights reserved. *Sweet Danger* (p251 of Penguin edition 1950). Marjorie Allingham's *Tiger in the Smoke* and *Sweet Danger* now available to buy in paperback from Vintage, Random House, UK.

Raymond Chandler: *Farewell My Lovely*, (Page 10, Folio edition published 1989) published by Hamish Hamilton, London 1940 and *The Long Goodbye*, (pp 1 and 33 Folio edition 1989) published by Penguin Books, London 1959; copyright Penguin Books. Reproduced by permission of Penguin Books Ltd.

John Harvey: *Flesh & Blood*, (pp17 & 73, Arrow Books edition, 2005) published by William Heinemann, London, 2004. Reprinted by permission of the Random House Group Ltd.

Reginald Hill: *Good Morning Midnight* (p80, Avon Books edition, USA 2005), published by HarperCollins 2005. Reprinted by permission of HarperCollins Publishers Ltd

P D James: *Original Sin* (pp 9/10 & 24, Penguin edition 1996), published by Faber and Faber 1994, Copyright P D James 1994, Reproduced by permission of Greene & Heaton Ltd

Val McDermid: *The Last Temptation* (p 3 St Martin's Press paperbacks edition 2003), published HarperCollins 2002; *The Mermaids Singing*, (p1), published HarperCollins 1995; *The Wire In The Blood*, (p369), published HarperCollins 1997. All reprinted by permission of HarperCollins Publishers Ltd, London

Catriona MacPherson: *After The Armistice Ball*, (p15), published by Constable, an imprint of Constable & Robinson Ltd, London, 2005. Reprinted by permission of Constable & Robinson Ltd

Frank MacShane: Introduction to *Raymond Chandler: The Complete Novels*, published by The Folio Society, London, 1989, copyright Frank MacShane 1989. Reprinted by permission of The Folio Society

Denise Mina: *Garnethill*, (pp 15, 82/83, 341) published by Bantan Press, London, 1998, reprinted by permission of The Random House Group Ltd

Ian Rankin: *Fleshmarket Close* (pp 4/5, 231 Orion Paperback edition 2005) published Orion Fiction, a division of The Orion Publishing Group, London, 2004. *The Hanging Garden* (pp 11/12), published by Orion Fiction, a division of The Orion Publishing Group, London, 1998. Reprinted by permission of The Orion Publishing Group Ltd

C J Sansom: *Dark Fire* (pp5/6) published by Macmillan, London, 2004. Reprinted by permission of Macmillan Publishers Ltd

Dreda Say Mitchell: *Running Hot* (pp 7, 15/16) published by The Maia Press Ltd, London, 2004. Reprinted by permission of The Maia Press Ltd

Andrew Taylor: *American Boy* (p6) published by Flamingo, an imprint of HarperCollins Publishers, London, 2003. Reprinted by permission of HarperCollins Publishers Ltd

Barbara Vine: *A Fatal Inversion* (p1) published Viking, London. 1987. Copyright: Kingsmarkham Enterprises Ltd 1987. Reprinted by permission of PFD on behalf of Kingsmarkham Enterprises Ltd

Minette Walters: *The Breaker* (p7 Jove Books, New York, 2000) published Macmillan, London, 1992. Reprinted by permission of Macmillan Publishers Ltd

Laura Wilson: *Dying Voices* (pp 3, 172 Orion Paperback edition 2001) published by Orion Fiction, a division of The Orion Publishing Group, London, 2000. Reprinted by permission of The Orion Publishing Group.

Robert Wilson: *A Small Death in Lisbon,* (pp 384, 515/516 HarperCollins Paperback edition) published by HarperCollins 1999. Reprinted by permission of HarperCollins Publishers Ltd

Index

adventure novels, 19
Allingham, Margery, xiii, 37, 109, 152, 169
amateur sleuth, 23, 82–
approaches (in crime novels), 19
Arnott, Jake, 26

backgrounds, 81–
Baker, John, 171
Barry, Michael, 87
Baverstock, Alison, 182
Bazalgette, Peter, 85
Billingham, Mark, 22, 43
Brett, Simon, 82
Burke, James Lee, 20

categories (of crime novels), 19–28
Chandler, Raymond, xiv, 20, 97, 109, 136, 140
chapter hooks, 132/133
characterisation, 49–64
Christie, Agatha, xiii, xv, 39, 144, 151, 169
Clancy, Tom, 19
Cleverly, Barbara, 180
clues, 124–129
Coben, Harlan, 14, 149
Collins, Wilkie, xiii
Collins, Michael, 22
comic crime novels, 23
conflict, 6, 39, 86–
Connolly, John, 20
Cooper, Natasha, 21, 56, 132, 135, 155
Cornwell, Patricia, 27, 144
crime novel, definition of, xiv–xv
  categories of, 19–23
Cutler, Judith, 82, 94, 124
CWA, 180/1

Davis, Lindsey, xvii, 20, 160
Debut Dagger, 180
Denby, Joolz, 180

denouements, 143–153
Dexter, Colin, 40, 81
dialogue, 67–79
Dibdin, Michael, 171
Dostoevsky, xiii

Eddy, Paul, 19
editing, 135–1
Edwards, Martin, xvii, 46, 53, 83, 84, 113
Edwards, Ruth Dudley, 20, 47, 170, 183
endings, 143–153
Evanovich, Janet, 20
Evans, Liz, xvii
exercises, 3, 6, 11, 13, 16, 24, 26, 33, 40, 44, 46, 50, 53, 67, 70, 72, 79, 87, 95, 101, 104, 108, 112, 118, 121, 123, 129, 133, 136, 149, 158, 167, 180

fairy tales, use of, 12–13
first paragraphs, 107–112
focus, 115–118
Forbes, Colin, 19
forensic science, 90–93, 164/6
Forster, E M, 1
Francis, Dick, 25, 148, 171

Gash, Jonathan, 82
Gilbert, Michael, 84
Goddard, Robert, 14, 149
Gosling, Paula, xvii
Grafton, Sue, 21, 97, 124
Granger, Ann, 30, 49, 83, 137, 164
Grant-Adamson, Lesley, 84
Gray, Alex, 43, 49, 113, 155
Grisham, John, 21
Gutteridge, Peter, 20

Hale, Hilary, xvi
Hammett, Dashiel, xiv
hardboiled crime novels, 23, 25
Harvey, John, 71, 102, 125

Hill, Reginald, 1, 22, 38, 73, 93, 99, 122, 134
historical crime novels, 23
Horton, Lesley, 43

ideas, 1
internet, 161/2, 181
issues, 43–47

James, P D, 37, 38, 42, 68, 81, 91, 171
James, Russell, 14, 84
Jardine, Quinton, 82
Jecks, Michael, xvii, 20, 29, 59, 157, 159, 173, 183

Keating, HRF, 1
Kernick, Simon, 22, 43, 94

legal crime novels, 23
length, 169
Leonard, Elmore, xiv
Lock, Joan, 163/4
London Library, 160/161
Lovesey, Peter, xvii, 2, 16, 20, 28, 71, 120, 138, 140, 170/1, 173, 183
Lovesey, Phil, 22

McBain, Ed, xiv, 22, 94
Macshane, Frank, 98
McDermid, Val, 20 21, 37, 38, 40, 43, 53, 109, 121, 145, 165
MacDonald, John D, 37
McGown, Jill, 22, 153
Malcolm, John, 46, 82, 86, 124
Mann, Jessica, 1, 83, 149
manuscript checks, 172/3
 format, 173/5
Marsh, Ngaio, xiii, xiv
Marsters, Priscilla, 23
Marston, Edward, xvi
medical details, 161/2
Miles, Keith, xvi, xvii, 15, 21, 43, 56, 63, 71, 79, 164

Mina, Denise, 22, 23, 44, 58, 74, 81, 88/89, 100, 171
Mitchell, Dreda Say, 111, 157, 175
Moody, Susan, 62, 101, 122
Moseley, Walter, 20
motivation, 12, 49–64
murder methods, 87–93
Murphy, Margaret, 22, 171

narration, 97–106
news media, use of, 8, 10–12

outlines, 28–35

pace, 133–141
Paretsky, Sue, 21, 97
pictures, 166/7
plotting 1–17
Poe, Edgar Allan, xiii
point of view, 97, 118–
poison, 92/93
police procedural novels, 23, 26, 93–95
police procedure, 162
Private Eye novel, 23
psychological crime novels, 23, 25

questions, 132/3

Rankin, Ian, xvi, xvi, xvi, 22, 38, 43, 57, 68, 83, 89, 94, 115, 148
red herrings, 128/129
Reichs, Kathy 27, 91
Rendell, Ruth, 93, 111, 172, 182
research, 155–
Rhea, Nicholas, 8, 38
Ridpath, Michael, 82

Sansom, C J, 20, 76
Sayers, Dorothy, xiii, 125
Saylor, Steven, 20
self-publishing, 181/2
selling your book, 175
series characters, 81–84, 123/124
settings, 37–42

Sharp, Zoe, 24, 84
specialised knowledge, 9, 16, 81–95, 160
Spring, Michelle, 23
style, 106/107
sub-plots, 15–16, 149
suspects, 52, 122/123
Symons, Julian, 90

Taylor, Andrew, 20, 38, 76, 77, 135, 169
Thomas, Edwin, 180
titles, 170
Tope, Rebecca, 84
traditional crime novels, 23, 26
Turner, Sarah, 135

verification, 168
Vine, Barbara, 111, 148, 172
voices from the grave, 120–122

Walker, Peter N, 8, 38, 63, 165
Wallis Martin, J, 22
Walters, Minette, 22, 44, 52, 110, 122
Welsh, Louise, 113
Wetton, Steve, 13
Wilson, Laura, 58, 110, 150
Wilson, Robert, 14, 73, 126
writers' handbooks, 175, 181